T0208366

THE ABCs OF APA STYLE

THE ABCs OF APA STYLE

Beth Lee

ARCHWAY
PUBLISHING

This content is not a substitute for the *Publication Manual of the American Psychological Association, 6ᵗʰ Edition* (2010), which contains comprehensive and authoritative guidance on all aspects of scientific writing.

APA has a number of resources to help individuals learn APA style, including free tutorials, FAQs, and APA Style blog. Visit http://www.apastyle. org/ for more information, and join APA Style on Facebook http://www. facebook.com/APAStyle and Twitter http://twitter.com/#!/APA_Style.

Archway Publishing books may be ordered through booksellers or by contacting:

Archway Publishing
1663 Liberty Drive
Bloomington, IN 47403
www.archwaypublishing.com
1 (888) 242-5904

ISBN: 978-1-4808-4602-9 (sc)
ISBN: 978-1-4808-4600-5 (hc)
ISBN: 978-1-4808-4601-2 (e)

Library of Congress Control Number: 2017908715

Print information available on the last page.

Archway Publishing rev. date: 08/29/2017

CONTENTS

INTRODUCTION

~~~~~~

Imagine yourself sitting in a classroom. Your professor hands out a piece of paper, explaining the requirements for a research paper. He or she goes through the list quickly. Yeah! You have an idea already! Great! Then, as you are leaving, he says, "By the way, you need to use APA." In a slight panic, you look around you. Everyone—yes, everyone else—looks calm. They're all chatting casually with each other. Did you miss something? Are you stuck in one of those dreams where you haven't gone to class all term and now have a final that you forgot to study for? You want to ask, "What's APA?" Since you feel silly, you don't ask. What does that mean? What do you do?

So, you run back to your dorm room or apartment or bedroom at your parents' house and try to figure it out. You Google "APA" and get millions of results, and by that, I mean millions. (Go ahead and Google it. I dare you!)

You start to madly tear apart your room, looking for a book about APA (or something) that you had to buy for a class last year. You can't find it. Did you sell it back? Oh, man. Wait, you find it. The book is long and filled with lists. Oh, no. What now? There's too much information, and none of it makes sense. You have to use APA, but you have no idea what to do or how to use it. What now?

That's where I come in. (Nice to meet you, by the way, and thanks for buying my book!) I've been teaching APA Style formatting for many years, and as an instructor of both Comp I and Comp II classes (as well as many other classes, but the general focus in these classes is on learning how to write with APA Style in those two classes), I can tell you this little secret: very few students understand how to write using APA Style. You are *not* the only one.

Each term, a few students will look at me in stunned silence or post their confusion to the discussion board. *What is APA? How do I use it? Can't I just use MLA? That's what I've used before.* Every term my response it the same: No, you can't use MLA in this class. If you are confused, at least five other students in your class are also completely befuddled.

It's not uncommon to not have used APA Style in high school or prior to a freshman-level college composition class. I focus on teaching it as a main component of the research essay. Not all professors or instructors find it as important to teach as I do. In my classroom, if you are confused at the beginning of the term, by the end, you will have a working understanding of it—if not a good handle on "the author-date" format. Unfortunately, I don't have the honor of having you in my classroom, unless you attend the university where I teach. However, I did write this book so that you, too, would learn how to use APA Style in an easy-to-understand format, making it easier than the traditional textbook to gain an understanding of the rules and guidelines.

The reality is that if your school, professor, instructor, or teacher requires it, you need to learn the basic rules of APA Style. First, you really should have some understanding of how the parts all work together. Once you understand that, you can learn the rules. At the very least, you can move onto using the style guides and understand how to look up the information you need. That's okay too.

It would be great if we could all just copy and paste web addresses into our essays, wouldn't it? That's not how APA Style works. There is no style that lets you copy and paste web addresses into essays. (Maybe you could invent one. That sure would make it easier on everyone!) As it turns out, not every source comes from a website. We still use these crazy old inventions called books, and they don't always download onto your Kindle. Sometimes you have to take them off a shelf and use your hands to page through them. It's actually quite fun, if you're into that sort of thing. And there is something called a *DOI number* that is used in place of web addresses since web addresses can change with the wind.

While we are waiting for someone to invent a new formatting style, you will have to use APA Style. After all, that paper is due next week. You still don't understand what APA Style is—and nobody else around you seems to know either? That's why I'm here. How lucky are you? I will walk you through the different steps for formatting your essay and incorporating APA Style into your research. First, you need to take detailed notes about your research.

- Is your research a book, website, journal, or something else? What is the title?
- What is the title of the article?
- Who is the author or authors—with first and last names?
- When was it published (month, day, and year)?
- Who published it?
- What are the page numbers?
- What are the paragraph numbers?
- What is the name of the website/organization that published it?
- What is the web address?

The amount of information you find in each source will depend on the type of source you are researching/citing. For instance, a print book will obviously not have a web address, and an online book won't require the city and state of publication. Still, it's extremely important to gather as much information as possible. It will save you a tremendous amount of time to note all of this information with the notes you take for your research.

While this book won't be focused on note taking, it's important to gather pertinent details as you research. And if you are a thorough researcher, you won't have to go back to find those sources again because you forgot to get an author, page number, paragraph number, or date of publication. That's wasted time in a world where we already have precious little time.

RESEARCH SOURCES CHECKLIST

- title of book
- title of article
- author(s)
- editors(s)
- publication date (year, month, day)
- publication, state, city, and house
- page or paragraph numbers
- name of website or organization
- web address or DOI number

Before you go any further, I suggest opening a Word document and starting a list that looks something like this:

LIST OF RESOURCES

First Source:

- author(s) and editor(s) names (first/last)
- title of article
- title of book or journal
- publication date
- page numbers/paragraphs
- web address or DOI number
- place of publication

I created a document called *Research Notes Format*, which is located at the end of this book. You can use to help you as you begin your research. It asks for the information above and gives you some space to take notes.

With the above information for each of your sources, you are can write an APA citation, and complete your *References* page. (I know, you may not understand quite what this means yet, but you will. I promise.) You thought it was more complicated than that, didn't you? Well, it is, but only slightly! Once you understand the basics, you can cite any book, journal, magazine, reliable website, or newspaper—both in print and online (except for the print website, because, you know, that won't exist.)

What's interesting is that during the course of my research for this book, I found much information that was incorrect. Most of the information or examples were off by a hair, meaning they might have missed a comma or placed a period in the wrong place—small but interesting mistakes. Frankly, without having written this book, I never would have noticed there were mistakes.

I only point this out as a curious fact and to hopefully make you feel better if you bought this book because you don't understand APA Style formatting. Now, having stated this, I'm not condoning not putting your best foot forward. I believe the mistakes I found did not negate the effort put forth. However, I want to mention the three best sources of information for once you have read and understood how to cite using APA Formatting in this book. We are only covering the basics and the most common types of sources you will be citing in the course of your research during the first couple of years in college (or the last couple of years in high school). Eventually, you might need additional information. For instance, I'm not going to discuss how to cite a statute (or legislative matters of any kind), executive materials, or collections from archives. At some point in your college career, you may need to know how to cite these items. When you do, I recommend the most reliable sources available:

1. Apastyle.org's blog: http://blog.apastyle.org/
2. *Publication Manual of the American Psychological Association* (this can be found in print and e-book formats)
3. Purdue's OWL (online writing lab): https://owl.english.purdue.edu/

Rather than using *Publication Manual of the American Psychological Association* throughout this book, I will refer to it as APA's *Publication Manual* or simply the *Publication Manual*.

The first two are from the horse's mouth, so to speak. APA's *Publication Manual* is the most comprehensive book, and lists any type of source you could possibly imagine. The apastyle.org's blog is the website where you can purchase the manual. However, its blog also has an abundance of free material about citing sources, both in text and in your References page. Lastly, the Purdue OWL and I have been friends for many, many years. I have used it regularly over the years as a helpful teaching tool.

The OWL, Purdue University's online writing lab, is one of the best resources you will find anywhere for anything grammar- and research essay-related—hands down. And it's a completely free resource to everyone (as is the apastyle.org's blog). You will have to purchase or borrow a copy of the *Publication Manual* if you want to use it. Most Comp I and Comp II textbooks have at least one chapter dedicated to APA Style. If you're lucky, a professor or instructor might hand out a cheat sheet for APA Style. However, since they are usually just lists, you'll still need to understand the rules in order write your in-text citations and reference page.

Because this is a book for beginners, it will cover the most basics of APA Style. You will need to understand four main parts—and you will understand them once you have completed this book:

- formatting your essay in APA Style
- writing in-text citations
- writing your References page
- mechanics and usage

Once you really understand how these main elements work, you can move onto using the more complex style guides and other reference materials. Since you are a beginner, you don't yet need to learn about some of the other elements. Some of the elements of APA Style are for scientists, methodologists, and those who do research for a living. If you fit into one of those categories, you need a different book. You should already know this!

CHAPTER 1

What is APA Style?

A citation is both a signpost and an acknowledgment. As a signpost, it signals the location of your source. As an acknowledgment, it reveals that you are indebted to that source. (Hunter, 2013, p. 1)

In response to a demand for standards in publishing, a group of professionals established rules and procedures for publishing documents in several fields, including psychologists and anthropologists. This group called itself the American Psychological Association, also known as APA (APA, 2012). So, in other words, the APA was conceived in order to establish standards for publication and written communications, basically in the social sciences, humanities, and business.

THE FUNDAMENTALS

- For the purposes of this book, when "style" is referred to, it does not mean voice, tone, or grammar. APA Style is a proper noun, and it is the way we cite our sources and format research essays.

- Citing sources means simply telling your reader where you found your information.
- There are three main types of formatting you will use in college: APA Style, MLA Style, and Chicago Style. They are distinct and are used in different disciplines.
- Always use italics when citing the name of a textbook or journal.
- If you don't know what style to use in your essay, ask your instructor or professor.
- This book will focus on APA Style formatting, in-text citations, the References page, and the rules of mechanics.

AUTHOR'S ASIDE

Are you a *Seinfeld* fan? Even if you're not old enough to remember them in first run, it's on in reruns all the time. Okay, slight exaggeration, but if you're not into reruns on TV, I know you can watch in on Roku. However, you don't need to. I'm going to use a reference to it to make a point about this book. In the episode "The Opposite," Kramer is on a book tour. His coffee table book turns *into* a coffee table. Clever, right? It's the same with this book! However, since this book is about APA Style, the in-text citations are written in APA Style. So, it's the coffee table book that turns into a coffee table. Sort of. However, if you get stuck, or start to understand APA Style, use this book as an example. Or the "Quick Reference and Essay Example" in the "A Closer Look" section of this book. I'm going to cite the *Seinfeld* episode now (David, Cowan, & Seinfeld, 1994.)

Did you try to Google APA Style yet? If not, I will tell you that you will get more than 19 million hits. With the advent of the Internet, the rules have gotten (only) slightly more complicated than they were when they began. I'm kidding. They've gotten significantly more complicated. Consider this: when the first style guide came out in 1929, it was only seven pages long! And today, the American Psychological

Association's (APA, 2012) *Publication Manual* is nearly three hundred pages long!

The main reason that APA and other styles of formatting have had to revise their style guides is because of the use of the Internet in research. Believe it or not, when the Internet became popular in the 1990s, most educational institutions refused to consider any information on it as anything more than rumor and hokum. The first search engine had the same name as a popular comic book character, for goodness sake. How could the academic world take something named Archie seriously?

However, here we are, more than twenty years later, and the Internet is likely the main source of research for most students. Today, most colleges and universities have awesome online libraries, so you can actually do your research in your jammies at midnight if you want to. And you can drink juice. In an actual library, you can't drink juice. Don't underestimate the brick and mortar library located at your college or university though. At some point, you might need to look at a print source or talk to a librarian who can help point you in the direction of some article or piece of research that you might need for a particular assignment. Not all valuable resources are online, and not all online information is useful.

Whether you are visiting an actual library or researching in a virtual one, the basic rules of research are still the same: For every instance in your research essay that you do not use common knowledge or your own thoughts, you must cite your source. Citing your source is simply crediting the information you borrowed back to its original source. Tell the reader where you found the information. If not, you have a whole world of trouble on your hands in the form of plagiarism. I'm not going to spend time lecturing you about plagiarism. You should know what it is and how to avoid it. It is safe to say that if you cite your sources, then everyone is happy!

Are you wondering what other styles of formatting exist? There are several types of formatting, but in general, only two others are used in undergraduate academia. They are MLA Style and Chicago

Style. It's important to understand a little bit about the other two because there are differences between all of them; some are significant, and some are very subtle. This book will discuss the differences and similarities between the styles and then move back to APA Style.

APA STYLE

APA Style was created in 1929 by a group that primarily consisted of psychologists. APA is short for American Psychological Association. It is not only psychiatrists who designed the guidelines for and writing using APA Style formatting. According to Purdue's online writing lab, OWL, it is primarily used in the social sciences. If you're in college or at a university, this means that you will write in APA style for almost all classes that fall under that category: communications, anthropology, psychology, sociology, economics, and many more. If your instructor or professor doesn't tell you what style to use, go ahead and ask. It will likely be APA.

KEY CONCEPTS ABOUT APA

- APA style includes a title page.
- You should have a running head at the top of each page of your essay.
- It is double-spaced throughout.
- In-text citations include author (or title), date of publication, and sometimes page numbers.
- The References page lists all the information from your in-text citations in greater detail.

We will go over all of this in much greater detail in the formatting sections of this book. This is meant as a very brief overview so you can see how APA compares to MLA and Chicago Style.

Unless you are familiar with APA Style, which you probably are not since you are reading this book, you probably don't know what a running head is. The running head appears on every page of your essay and is the title or shortened title of your essay. If your title is more than six or eight words, go ahead and shorten it for the running head. Apastyle.org suggests that you not use more than fifty characters. Before the title, you should always add "Running Head" ("Quick Answers," 2014).

This is what your running head will look like:

Running Head: The ABC's of APA   1

The ABC's of APA

Beth Lee

Bartridge College

MLA

MLA, which stands for Modern Language Association, is almost exclusively used in the humanities, mostly for writing research about literature and language ("What is MLA Style," 2014).

KEY CONCEPTS ABOUT MLA

- It's double-spaced throughout.
- It does not have a cover page. Rather, you include your name, instructor/professor's name, class, and date (in that order) left-justified at the top of the essay's first page. The title is next, center-justified.
- You begin the essay after the title.
- There is a header in the upper right-hand corner than runs throughout the essay (except the first page.)

This is what your first page looks like:

Beth Lee

Professor Layperson

English 123

15 January 2016

MLA Formatting

Your double-spaced essay begins here. As you know, you should always begin your essay with a 'hook.' This is an interesting fact, anecdote, statistic or quote that invites your audience to continue reading. What is it about your topic that you could tickle your readers' interest and keep that interest going? Once you do that, you want to introduce your topic. You should always end the introductory paragraph with a thesis, which is a roadmap to the essay's body.

- In-text citations vary from APA Style in that there aren't commas—and MLA relies on author and page numbers rather than publication dates.
- MLA essays have a works cited page, whereas APA has a References page. There are slight differences, but they are not important since we will discuss the References page in great detail in a later chapter. However, *don't* add a works cited page

to your APA Style essay (Russel, Brizee, Angeli, Keck, and Paiz, 2014, paras. 15–24).

- Always italicize the titles of books and journals.

THE CHICAGO MANUAL OF STYLE

Chicago Style is another common way to cite outside sources in a research essay. Chicago style is used in varying subjects, but most often, you will find it used in journalism and publishing. If you are in those fields, you will likely use Chicago Style. However, you may, later in life, publish a book or an article in a newspaper, textbook, book, or journal. Many editors prefer Chicago Style. It is the most different from APA and MLA.

KEY CONCEPTS ABOUT CHICAGO STYLE

- You double-space throughout.
- Chicago Style has a cover page, but it is formatted differently from APA Style essays.
- Chicago Style uses a number and notes system for in-text citations.
- Chicago Style uses a bibliography. If you are writing an APA Style essay, don't use a bibliography. Bibliography is for Chicago Style.
- Always italicize the titles of books and journals.

These are the biggest highlights. Since we are concentrating on the differences between the three styles, it's best not to go into more detail than necessary about the different styles.

THE BIG IDEA

- APA was formed in 1929 and was only seven pages long! Today, the manual is nearly three hundred pages.
- The focus of this book is on formatting, in-text citations, the References page, and the rules of mechanics.
- Books, journals, and web pages are the most common types of sources that beginning writers of APA Style use.
- There are three main styles for formatting research essays: APA Style, MLA, and Chicago Style. They all have subtle differences.
- The importance of understanding the differences between APA Style, MLA, and Chicago Style is to understand what *not* to put into your APA Style essay. While some of the differences are slight, they are extremely important.
- Double-space all research essays—no matter which style you choose.
- Always italicize the titles of books, journals, and newspapers.

CHAPTER 2

The Key Aspects of APA Style

I tell a student that the most important class you can take is technique. A great chef is first a great technician. If you are a jeweler, or a surgeon or a cook, you have to know the trade in your hand. You have to learn the process. You learn it through endless repetition until it belongs to you. ("Jacques Pepin quotes," n. d.)

THE FUNDAMENTALS

- Don't plagiarize. It is bad karma, and all colleges and universities have academic honesty policies that have repercussions from failing the essay to expulsion.
- There are four key elements you need to consider when working with APA Style: formatting, rules of mechanics, in-text citations, and the References page.
- Even if you are not writing a research essay, you can still format an essay in APA Style.
- In-text citations tell the reader the author (or title), the date, and the page or paragraph number of your source.

- The References page has more information about your source if your reader wants to find it and do more reading about the subject.
- What do you call it when you don't cite your sources in the text or in the References page? Plagiarism.

Before you begin reading further, plagiarism is taken very seriously in academics—and I urge you not to do it. If you use another person's thoughts, ideas, words, or expressions, that's plagiarism. I've been an instructor for a long time, and fortunately, I've only come up against it a few times. In one instance, a student bought another essay and turned it in as his own. In another, a student copied and pasted directly from the Internet. Both students left equally bad trails. One student failed the essay. I had to have the other student removed from my class because she had done it before and had been formally warned. I felt sick about doing it both times.

Don't commit plagiarism. Cite your sources—even if you make a mistake. I've never failed a student who tried his or her best and did his or her own work. Never. And I am not about to now. I think most instructors and professors will be lenient (but might take points off) if your paper isn't perfectly formatted.

However, always put your best foot forward, do the assignment, and try your hardest to succeed. Get into the habit of doing APA formatting correctly. The higher the level of class, the more your instructor will demand of you.

PLAGIARISM

Merriam Webster defines plagiarism as "the act of using another person's words or ideas without giving credit to that person" ("plagiarism," n. d.).

It's possible you've written an essay about plagiarism. It's not uncommon for one of the first essays you write in a Comp I or even a Comp II class to be about plagiarism. It's actually a fairly smart technique. It forces you to both try to format a research essay and understand what committing plagiarism can mean for your academic career. I'm not going to spend a lot of time discussing it. Buying a paper, copying and pasting from the Internet, and putting your name to it—or not citing sources you used in your essay—are all forms of plagiarism. There are more, but those are among the most severe and can get you expelled from school.

The basic rule of thumb is to remember this: If it's not your own words or common knowledge and you don't cite it, that's plagiarism. Common knowledge is knowledge you can expect most people to know. For instance, most people know that George Washington was the first president of the United States of America. Most people know that D-Day was on June 6, 1944. And most people know you need to have some sort of legal picture ID in order to board an airplane. Not everyone knows that Sioux Falls, South Dakota, has a population 162,300. If I tell you that information, I need to cite it properly—just like this: ("About Sioux Falls," 2014, para. 2.). I think that plagiarism should fall under common knowledge since we are more aware of it than ever in academia. In fact, my adorable twin boys are learning about it in the seventh grade.

If you cite your sources properly and ensure they are on the References page, then you've not committed plagiarism and are ready to move on to the next phase of your essay—proofreading. I'm not going to discuss proofreading here, but we still have a lot to talk about!

KEY POINT

In order to really understand APA Style formatting, you need to understand the three most important elements, which is what we will be discussing in the rest of the book. If you can get these three basics down, then you will be able to use the APA Style guide for more complex APA formatting. They are:

- formatting
- in-text citations

- the References page
- rules of mechanics

FORMATTING

Your professor or instructor might assign an assignment that doesn't require any research. For instance, this could be a personal narrative, a comparison/contrast essay, or an assignment that requires you to respond to questions from your textbook readings. However, he or she might add, "Make sure you use APA Formatting."

Even if you aren't writing a research essay, you still must follow some basic formatting guidelines. We will talk about these in greater detail in a later chapter.

IN-TEXT CITATIONS

When you write a research essay, you use paraphrasing, summarizing, and quotations from outside sources to support your ideas or argument. As I stated in the plagiarism section, any information that you find in outside sources that are not your own thoughts, ideas, or words—or is not common knowledge—must be cited. What's common knowledge? Common knowledge is information that most people know. For instance, most people know that George Washington was our first president. The general rule of thumb is to cite a source if you don't know the information yourself.

KEY POINT

Cite a source. You need to tell your reader, very briefly, some information about any outside source you cite. This can include words, ideas, information, graphs, photos, and images. Within the body of your research essay, you will indicate this with some information within parenthesis after you cite the information. For instance, I summarized a bit of information from another source for this paragraph, so I am going to cite it now ("About Citations," n. d. para. 1).

Your in-text citations will always include the following information:

- author (or title if there is no author listed)
- year of publication
- chapter, page, or paragraph numbers (depending on the source)

What do you now know about this source: ("About Citations," n. d. para. 1)? You know that there is no author because none is listed. You know there is *no date of publication* listed (hence the n. d.), and you know the information will be found on paragraph 1 of a website. If you want to find the website, it will be listed in the References page under "About Citations." You will become more familiar with this when we really begin to discuss in-text citations in a later chapter.

KEY POINT

The in-text citation tells you what to look up in the References page for further information about finding your outside source. The in-text citation just tells the reader "Hey, use the title or author from here and look it up in alphabetical order on your References page to find out more about where the writer found his or her information." It's just the shout-out to your References page. They're pals who work together—like Bert and Ernie.

REFERENCES

The in-text citations just tell readers where to look for more information in the References page, and the References page gives the reader the following information:

- author
- title
- publication date(s)
- page, paragraph, and chapter numbers
- publisher's name and place
- website where the information was found

Readers can use this information to find the outside source of information themselves. It is simply an alphabetical list of your outside sources.

It's important to note that if you do *not* cite a source within the essay, you do not need to add it to the References page. If you refer to a book, article, or website but don't actually use any of that information in the essay, you do not need to cite it. It's also not uncommon for someone to panic and add sources to the References page to meet a specific number of outside sources required for an essay. If there are a required number of sources, your professor will figure out if you pad the References page.

Not all the information listed above will be in the References page. For instance, a website won't have a publishing house. And some books, such as reference books, might not have an author. However, you need to gather as much information as you can for your reader and list it here. There are specific formatting guidelines for the References page, which we will discuss in further detail in a later chapter.

THE BIG PICTURE

- Don't commit plagiarism. It's really bad for your educational career—and could possibly end it.
- If you use an outside source, cite it. This means whether you paraphrase, summarize, or quote, it should always be cited.
- The only time you don't need to cite sources is if you use your own words, thoughts, or ideas—or if you use common knowledge.

The three most important parts of an APA Style essay are:

- formatting
- in-text citations
- References page

Even if you don't write a research essay, you can use APA Style formatting.

- The in-text citation is a parenthetical note that tells the reader where to find more information about your outside source in the References page. It's the shout-out to the References page.
- The References page includes a detailed, alphabetical list of all the outside sources you cited in the body of your essay.

CHAPTER 3

Formatting Your APA Style Essay

Some people, when faced with the technical preciseness required by a stylesheet, might stop and ask, "What's the big deal?" or "Isn't the writing more important than the formatting?" While it's true that stylesheet formatting is only one aspect of the complex task of research writing, it is an important one. Correct formatting can be the difference between a job done and a job done well. ("APA Reference Style: Introduction," 2002, para 3.)

THE FUNDAMENTALS

- You do not need to write a research essay in order to format your essay in APA Style. There are still some rules you should follow!
- Always double-space throughout your APA style essay. That's the number one rule in APA formatting.
- The abstract is often not mandatory in lower-level college and university class essays. Ask your instructor or professor if you need to add one.

- If you are not writing a research essay, you do not need to use in-text citations or a References page. They are only for citing outside sources.
- Always use plain, white 8.5 x 11-inch paper. Boring old white paper. Your essay will rely on your writing and research to make it interesting.
- Use an easy-to-read font, such as Arial or Times New Roman. (In higher level courses, this may become a more 'sticky issue.' As a beginner, while this is a rule, it isn't hard and fast, in my opinion. I never deduct points for the font, as long as it is easy to read. And for ease of use and aesthetics, I am using the same font throughout this textbook.)
- Double-space the essay in its entirety—from the title to the last line of the References page. No exceptions.
- Include a running head with the title and a page number throughout the essay. ("RUNNING HEAD" will appear on the title page of your essay in the header—but not in the remainder of the essay.

What do you do if your professor or instructor said you did not need to do any research for your compare/contrast essay, but you still need to use APA Style formatting? That's actually very smart of him. (He probably has a PhD, so I would guess he's a pretty smart fellow.) It's actually good news for you, too, because you can practice writing your essay without worrying about in-text citations and a References page. What does an APA Style essay look like without in-text citations and a References page? It looks fairly similar to a research essay. If that's the way your professor likes it, just go ahead and do it!

PLAIN WHITE PAPER

I cannot emphasize this with enough arm flailing and yelling: Don't use colored paper. (I'm actually jumping up and down as you read this.) Don't add fancy graphics, designs, or photos to your title page. If you want to add a graph or photo to emphasize a point in your essay, that's acceptable. However, you should not add them to add "content" to your essay so that it meets your length requirement.

If your professor designates a three-to-five-page paper, you should have three full, double-spaced pages of content. Once you have added enough content, you can add graphics, if they further a point or argument in your essay (and have been approved by your instructor or professor). In addition, avoid using long quotes just to add length to your essay. No three-page paper should have more than one long quote. That's an old trick that every instructor and professor in the country has seen, and it could cost you points in your final essay grade.

SPACING

Your entire essay, from the title page through the References page, should be double-spaced on standard 8.5 x 11-inch paper. This is good news because it's a pain in the butt to try to print anything on paper that's not standard size; you'd have to mess with all kinds of settings. I'm not sure how you will set your program to double-space, but it's fairly simple in Microsoft Word:

1. Right click on your mouse or your track pad on your laptop.
2. Choose Paragraph.
3. Choose Double.
4. Click Apply.
5. Voila. Your essay is set to double space. Now, don't change it.

MARGINS AND SPACES AND TAB—OH MY!

"One inch all around" is the number one rule of formatting. The only information you need to remember is this: an inch at the top, the bottom, to the left, and to the right. Most word processors will have one-inch margins automatically set when you open up your software.

(It is the default for MS Word, specifically. Unless you messed with your margins and reset them for some weird reason—hey, that's your business—then you should be all set when you open it.)

Whenever you start a new paragraph, you should tab in five spaces, or half an inch. Most word processors (like MS Word) has a five-space, half-inch default, so all you will need to do is tab once every time you begin a new paragraph, and you are all set.

In the olden days, when typewriters were a hot commodity, people spaced twice between sentences. Well, it's not 1977 anymore, so we no longer do that. You should have single spacing between words throughout, including after an endnote. (An endnote is designated with a period or semicolon.)

This is an example of a correctly formatted essay with one-inch margins, proper tabs, and one space between sentences:

HISTORY OF HALLOWEEN

Over the last one hundred years, Halloween has become a holiday that focuses more on candy and celebrating and less on ghosts and goblins. Where once Halloween was a 'somber pagan ritual' it is now focused on having fun and creating a joyful experience ("Halloween," 2014, para. 1) In fact, Ankerberg has asserted that "Halloween symbols, customs, and practices undoubtedly have had a variety of influences upon Western culture throughout history," and was not a commonly observed until the twentieth century (2014, para. 3.)

RUNNING HEAD

Your essay requires a running head throughout the essay—from the title page to the last page of the reference page. The running head is located in the upper left-hand footer of your essay and appears on each page of your essay, including the References page. The title of your essay should appear on the running head if it is less than fifty characters. If it runs more than fifty characters, you should shorten in it a way that makes sense to your reader.

On the title page, you will have the words "RUNNING HEAD" preceding the title. The title is in all caps throughout the running head.

After the title page, you only need to use the title and should omit the words "running head."

Each subsequent page will only have the title. Interestingly, Purdue's OWL states that the most recent edition of the *Publication Manual of the American Psychological Association* has several errors (Angeli, 2014, para. 9). They posted a link to the corrections, which shows just what I've told you here in a sample essay posted by the APA (Leclerc & Kensinger, n. d.).

TITLE PAGE

All APA Style essays need a title. The general rule of thumb is to have it be less than twelve words and not more than two lines on the title page. The longer the essay, the more you might need to elaborate on the title, particularly if it is an essay in which you are explaining an experiment or methodology to support a thesis or results. However, generally speaking, for a three-to-five or five-to-eight-page paper, which is the general length of a college or university paper, you should use no more than twelve words.

Your title page includes the following:

- running head/title
- page number (top right, in header)
- title of paper
- your name (sometimes referred to as a byline)
- name of institution/college you are attending (or work for)

The running head and the page numbers should be placed in the header with one-inch margins. There isn't really a designation for how many spaces down you should begin the title. However, it's about one-third of the way down from the top of the paper. Double-spacing down three to four times should put you at about the right spot.

When assigning your essay a title, avoid this title: Paper No. 1—Narrative Essay. In fact, avoid giving your essay a number that coincides with the number of essays assigned in your class because it tells your reader no information about the contents of the essay. Put some thought into the title, whether you really want to or not. Think of something interesting and relevant; most readers will respond to a funny title. For some students, that's a very difficult task. For others, it's quite easy. Sometimes, the student is just being lazy. Let's face the facts here. Sometimes it's midnight and you're just glad to have the essay written. Whatever the reason, though, none of those are excuses for having a bad or thoughtless title. You want to tell your reader what the essay is about—but try to make it interesting.

You may not have wanted to write the essay. Heck, you may have hated it. That doesn't mean your audience has to suffer. This is your education. It is your time to shine. Show us how smart your mom has been telling you that you are all your life! I remember clever and interesting titles, and I often read the essay with a little more gusto than the essay titled "Research Paper #6," or "Cats versus Dogs" for a compare/contrast essay. I don't particularly want to read an essay titled "Argument Essay #5." Boring! Since you've bothered to write the essay, put a few extra minutes of thought into it. As your reader, I will certainly appreciate the effort. And if you can't be bothered to be clever, create a title that states the main idea of the essay. I might not love the title, but I won't hate it.

There are two more elements of formatting: the *Author Note* and the *Abstract*. Since this is a book for beginners, it's likely you'll never need to use either one until you have a better understanding of APA Style or are taking higher-level classes or conducting research. Nonetheless, since you might be asked to include one or both of these sections in your essays, I am going to cover them briefly here. If you don't know whether or not to include them, ask. It's better to be safe than sorry.

The author note is specifically written for articles that are submitted to scholarly journals. Generally, they are included in professional papers. The author note tells the reader certain information about the essay other than just the author and title. You will probably not ever use the author's note unless you are writing a paper about your own research or reporting findings of an experiment. Author's notes aren't even used much for theses and dissertations.

The author note contains the following information:

- The first paragraph includes the departmental information for each of the authors. The title page information tells the reader where the paper was researched and written. The Author Note includes affiliations by all the authors.
- The second paragraph will tell the reader if any of the authors have changed affiliations since the research was conducted or the essay was written.
- The third paragraph is much like the lady at the end of a PBS TV show (*History Detectives* is a personal favorite) who tells you what foundations and grants were used to create the program. Like public television, research at institutions must also be funded by outside sources.
- The last paragraph tells the reader who to contact about the paper (*APA*, 2010).

The author note looks like this:

The ABC's of APA

Beth Lee

Bartridge College

Author Note

Beth Lee, Department of English, Bartridge College

The research for this study was granted by Funding for APA Research, as well as private donations.

Correspondence concerning this article should be addressed to: Beth Lee, Department of English, 1212 North Drive, Bartridge College, Collegetown, IA, 55449. Email: author@bartridge.edu

Note the formatting. It's tabbed in for the first line and not tabbed in subsequent lines for each section.

ABSTRACT

Some professors or instructors might insist on an Abstract, and some may not. If you don't know whether to add an abstract, ask your instructor. Whether or not you should add one is going to depend on the level of class and the department. For instance, if you are writing a 400-level psychology class essay that's more than ten pages, an abstract is probably required. If it's a 100-level comparison/contrast three-page essay, an abstract is likely unnecessary.

If you don't know for sure whether or not to add one, you probably should write one, however brief it is. The general rule is that the abstract is designed to tell the reader what the paper is about. These are generally very long papers, scholarly papers, or papers that are submitted to scholarly journals. For a 100- or 200-level undergraduate class, your research essays are likely three-to-five pages or five-to-eight-pages, and abstracts aren't necessarily required. If you plan on writing scholarly papers or conducting research, writing Abstracts is a good habit to get into.

The abstract is a short but detailed summary of your paper. It's a way to let the reader know what is included before he or she reads the paper. The Abstract is alone on the second page of your paper (if you write one). It should be between 125 and 250 words in length. According to the *Publication Manual*, it should be "accurate, readable, and concise" (APA, 2010, p. 26). In layman's words, it's boring and emotionless, but it's a great way to practice your summary skills. And don't forget to write it last. Your paper should be completed in its entirety prior to writing the abstract.

REFERENCES PAGE AND IN-TEXT CITATIONS

THE BIG IDEA

- Your essay should be written on plain white 8.5 x 11-inch printer paper.
- Double-space your essay in its entirety. There are no exceptions to this rule.
- Do not add any embellishments to your essay.
- Use an easy-to-read sans format font. The most common is Times New Roman, but Calibri or Arial are also commonly used and accepted.
- The running head will state "RUNNING HEAD: Title" on the title page. On each page after that, you will only put the title in the running head.
- Your essay should have a page number in the upper right header of each page of your essay.
- The title page should include the title of your essay in twelve words or less, your name, and the name of the college or institution you belong to.

CHAPTER 4

In-Text Citations

WHY CITING IS IMPORTANT

It's important to cite sources you used in your research for several reasons:

- to show your reader you've done proper research by listing sources you used to get your information
- to be a responsible scholar by giving credit to other researchers and acknowledging their ideas
- to avoid plagiarism by quoting words and ideas used by other authors
- to allow your reader to track down the sources you used by citing them accurately in your paper by way of footnotes, a bibliography, or a reference list ("Why Citing is Important," n. d., para 1)

THE FUNDAMENTALS ~~~~~~~~~~~~~~~~~~~~

- In-text citations "point" to the References page, telling the reader where to find more information about your sources or where you found your research.
- For each in-text citation, there should be an entry in the References page.
- You need to properly cite the following information in an in-text citation:
  - author or title of article
  - year of publication
  - paragraph or page number
- If you don't have a title or author, you probably shouldn't use it as a source. If there isn't an author or a title, it's likely not a reliable source; therefore, you want to avoid using it in your essay.
- While the sequence of an in-text citation is the same for the quote, summary, and the paraphrase, the formatting is slightly different between the quote and the summary/paraphrase.
- A short quote uses quotation marks, while the long quote is formatted with a block quote.
- You will never, in any circumstances, use a website in your in-text citation. Never. If you use it, you are formatting your citations incorrectly.
- When you quote sources, be sure to use the exact words from your source.
- If you don't have an author, use the title.
- If you don't have a year of publication, use n. d, which stands for no date.
- If you don't have a page number, use the paragraph number.
- Use the word *and* between authors and editors for more than one author: Lee, B. and Smith, M. (1998) suggest that …

If you chose to read this book, you likely won't be searching archives for rare papers or studying scholarly papers by seven authors from 1983. Most of the research for essays will be completed at your college or school's on campus or online library, and online. Will you find journal articles written by more than three authors? You could. It's not likely for the type of research you will be doing in your current writing or 100- or 200-level classes. It makes the most sense to keep this beginner book as clean and simple as possible. You will have a much better understanding of the material.

You need to gather as much of the following information as you can during the course of your research because this information is necessary for in-text citations or the References page:

- author(s) name(s) and first initial(s)
- title of book, article, journal, or website
- date of publication (including month, day, and year)
- page and/or paragraph number(s)
- volume or edition number(s)
- city of publication
- publishing house
- DOI number
- web address

I recommend keeping track of this while you research so you won't be trying to find the information again when it's late at night and you are trying to put together the References page, especially if the paper is due in a few short hours and you procrastinated writing the essay. By staying organized during the research process, you will have a much easier time writing your in-text citations and References page.

You will need as much information as possible because you never use simply a website when citing your sources. Websites change, web sources can require log-ins, and other issues can arise over time. It's important to give your audience as much information about your source as is available. The more information, the likely the more credible your source is as well.

It's up to you how you take and organize your notes for writing your paper. (I really hope you take and organize your notes when you write your essays. If you don't, you really need to rethink your research skills.) There are many great websites that can help you create a *visual organizer*. This is simply a way to outline your essay as you research and begin to write it.

One method for staying organized that I suggest is putting everything into a carefully titled and organized Word document. For a beginner, it might look something like this:

- main point
- quote, summary, or paraphrase
- insert your main point here

CITATION INFORMATION

- author(s) last names and first initial(s)
- title of book, article, journal, or website
- date of publication (including month, day, and year)
- page (text) and/or paragraph number(s) (web)
- volume or edition number
- city of publication
- publishing house
- DOI number
- web address

Once you have organized your note taking, you can add whatever information you collect and erase whatever information you cannot find. For instance:

Main Point: Will there be a vaccine to prevent Alzheimer's?

Quote:

'Multiple major trials and hundreds of millions of dollars have been poured into research on passive vaccines, which is the dominant approach. [With passive vaccination, antibodies against a particular condition are given directly to a person.] In the past, there were very significant side effects in trials of active vaccine, and so there has been less interest in these in recent years. Having said that, there is one active vaccine in development with an upcoming trial, and tau vaccine trials are also coming in the not-too-distant future. These may all end up being complementary approaches.'

- o Author: Matt McMillen

- o Title of Web Article: Alzheimer's: The State of Prevention, Treatment

- o Date of publication: August, 20, 2014

- o Paragraph Number: 21

- o Web Address: http://blogs.webmd.com/breaking-news/2014/08/alzheimers-the-state-of-prevention-treatment.html

For the quote above, the information was taken from a WebMD article written by Mat McMillen. The article is entitled "Alzheimer's: The State of Prevention, Treatment" and was published on their website on August 20, 2014.

THE AUTHOR-DATE METHOD

The author-date method refers to in-text citations, and they are also included in the References page. In its simplest form, it looks like this:

IN-TEXT CITATIONS

Author (2014) states ...
(Author, year)

REFERENCES PAGE

Author, A. (Year).

There are three primary types of sources that are cited in research essays:

- quotations
- summaries
- paraphrases

THE AUTHOR-DATE METHOD

The order in which you document your in-text citations will be the same for quotations, summaries, and paraphrases. It's called the author-date method, and this is the information you will need to format your in-text citations:

- author's last name *or* title of article/book if there is no author listed
- year of publication *or* n. d. (no date)
- page number (book or journal) *or* paragraph number (web articles without page numbers)

You will always tell your reader who the author is first, followed by the year and page number. This is the order in which you will write each of your in-text citations, whether they are quotations, summaries, or paraphrases:

author/title // year or n. d // page or paragraph number

That's it. That's all the information you need for the *in-text citations*. However, you still need all the other information I talked about earlier in the chapter to build your References page, which we will discuss in the next chapter.

The way in which you format in-text citations will not change, but there are some variations for using quotes, summaries, and paraphrases. There are two reasons for this.

- Unlike a summary and paraphrase, if you quote material from your source, you must use quotation marks in a short quote. A short quote has forty words or less.
- A long quote is formatted differently than a short quote, summary, and paraphrase because you use the block method rather than quotation marks.

I want to emphasize again that you should *never* use a website in an in-text citation. You will not use a web address. Hopefully you never will. Any outside source you use needs to be reliable, credible, and trustworthy. And you need to ensure that your audience knows clearly who the author is. If you find sources that have no author or title, just skip them. Do not use them. If all you have is a website, either you haven't done your due diligence or your website is not reliable and you should dump it.

Ask your professor if using wiki pages is acceptable as a source. I do not allow my students to use anonymous sources in research essays. However, if you scroll down to the bottom and find the initial source of your wiki page, you might use that article. Having said that, some wiki sites are becoming more reliable for its content, so it's not as uncommon to source one now.

When you research your essay, you need to use only reliable sources. This means very simply that your sources must come from reliable websites (.edu, .gov, and .org) or reliable journals and books. It's up to you to decide. For the duration of this book, I will *only* refer to sources that have an author and/or a title. If you come across a website or source that has neither, then it's not going to be reliable and you should not use it.

Since this is a book for beginners, you are likely a beginning researcher as well. Ensuring that you have an author and/or title will make the research and writing process much easier. You won't find any information in this book that will help you cite a source without the author and/or title. You'll be wasting your time looking for it. Your professor or instructor will thank me later for that advice to you.

QUOTATIONS

There are two types of quotations:

- short quotations
- long quotations

When you take the exact words from your source, you always need to put them in quotes. However, you also must "frame" your quote by telling your reader what the point of the quote is. You can never just throw a quote into an article. You must always introduce it.

Framing, or introducing your quote, is done using the author-date method. You want to include the author and the year of publication for your source. If you don't have an author, use the title of the article you are quoting from.

Once you are ready to add the quote, you will need to set up the quote.

Use this decision tree to help you cite your short quotation:

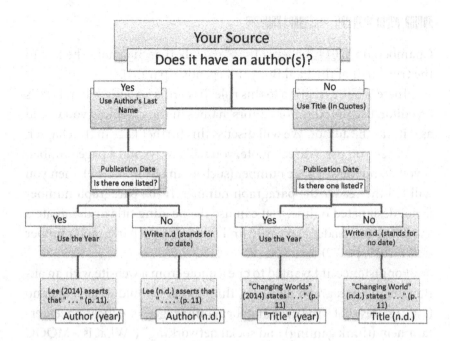

EXAMPLES OF THE MOST COMMON TYPES OF QUOTATION CITATIONS

AUTHOR, PUBLICATION DATE, PAGE NUMBERS

Drake (1983) maintains that "a poem of address is at the same time intimate and distant" (53).

AUTHOR, NO PUBLICATION DATE, PARAGRAPH NUMBERS

Author (n. d) states that "we can't go backwards, only forward" (para. X).

NO AUTHOR, PUBLICATION DATE, PAGE NUMBERS

Merriam Webster (2006) states that "to steal and pass off (the ideas or words of another) as one's own" is plagiarism (p. 965).

AUTHOR, PUBLICATION DATE, PARAGRAPH NUMBERS

Chamberlain (2014) believes that "Canada that may hold the key to the true birth of the Paul Bunyan Legends" (para. 2).

There is one exception to this rule: If there is no author, but there is an editor, use the editor or editors' names in the same way you would as if it was the author. We will discuss this further later in the chapter.

When you use a direct quote, you will always add a page number. If you do not have a page number (such as an online article), then you will tell the reader the paragraph number. If the paragraph number is not designated online, you can use the heading title or designate a short title the reader can easily find followed by a paragraph number (*APA*, 2010, p. 172).

For instance, if I wanted to cite a quote from a website with an author, but no paragraph numbers, this is what I would write: Pappano (2012) states that "The evolving form knits together education, entertainment (think gaming) and social networking" ("What is a MOOC Anyway," para 3).

The author is Pappano, and the article was published in 2012. I can find this particular quote in the third paragraph under the heading "What is a MOOC Anyway."

If you have multiple authors, you would follow the rules for multiple authors. If you have two authors, you would write: Author and Author state " ... " (p. xxx).

Johnson-Sheehan and Paine suggests that a "well-written paragraph keeps the readers' focus on a central subject" (p. 418).

Here is an example if there are three authors:

Author, Author & Author (year) maintain " ...." (p. x).

Brown, White, and Grey (2011) state, "The effects can still be felt today" (p. 2).

LONG QUOTES

If you have been assigned an essay that is longer than three pages long and want to add a long quote, you have to set it up as a block. A long quote is always more than forty words. A block quote is double-spaced and uses a half-inch tab for its entirety (*APA*, 2010). The general rule of thumb for block quotes is no more than one every three or more pages. Use them sparingly. Long quotes should only be used to support your argument or ideas. It should not be used as filler because you ran out of anything else to say.

Here are some quick rules for formatting your long quote:

- It is double-spaced throughout.
- Use a half-inch margin throughout.
- Use the author-year style for citing.
- Do *not* use quotation marks.
- Use the author-year-page number method for citations.
- You need to introduce your long quote. Tell the reader why you are putting this quote in the essay.

Here is a decision tree to help you cite your long quote:

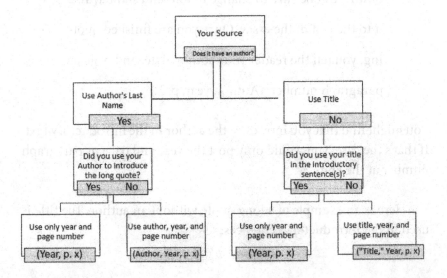

The following rules for citing are the same for the long quote as the short quote:

- If you do not have an author, you will use the title.
- If you don't know the date, use n. d. in place of the year.
- Multiple author rules also apply (McAdoo, 2013).

Let's look at some examples!

Here is an example of a long quote that does not use the author in the introductory sentence(s):

You will introduce your long quote to your reader by telling him why you are using this quote to support your ideas. Then, you will add a colon and begin the quote:

> You will use the exact words the author uses. You can copy and paste the entry in its entirety if your source is online. But be sure to change to font and standardize it to the rest of the essay. Once you are finished quoting, you tell the reader your author, date, and page or paragraph number. (Author, year, p. X)

You might find that you introduce the author in the introductory text. If that's the case, you would only post the year and page or paragraph number at the end.

Here is an example of a long quote without an author. The title is used in the introductory sentences:

You might think it's acceptable just to reprint a lengthy work from another author and cite that source. This could be a copyright infringement. The article "Facts about Dreaming" discusses why we dream:

> There are many theories about why we dream, but no one knows for sure. Some researchers say dreams have no purpose or meaning and are nonsensical activities of the sleeping brain. Others say dreams are necessary for mental, emotional, and physical health. (2016, para. 5)

Here is an example of a long quote with multiple authors used in the introductory sentence:

Johnson-Sheehan and Paine have written about collaborating on school projects. They maintain:

> Working in teams allows people to concentrate their personal strengths and take advantage of each other's abilities. Working with others also helps you to be more creative and take on larger and more complex projects. Computers and the Internet have significantly increased our ability to collaborate with others. (2013, p. 455)

Here is the same quote, but the authors are not introduced in the opening sentence:

One particular study found that:

> Working in teams allows people to concentrate their
> personal strengths and take advantage of each other's
> abilities. Working with others also helps you to be
> more creative and take on larger and more complex
> projects. Computers and the Internet have signifi-
> cantly increased our ability to collaborate with others.
> (Johnson-Sheehan & Paine, 2013, p. 455)

Do you see the pattern yet? Just remember that you only need to post three pieces of information in an in-text quotation citation: the author (or title), year of publication (or n. d.), and the page or paragraph number. For a summary and paraphrase, it's only the author (or title) and the year.

SUMMARY AND PARAPHRASE

Citing summaries and paraphrases in text are treated equally. This is because they are similar in style to one another. In its most general terms, a summary states a main point in a very shortened version of the original. For instance, I might summarize the novel *Gone Girl* by Gillian Flynn (2012) as the ultimate story of revenge. I succinctly summarized an entire novel in only a few words. That's how you summarize. (Because I summarized the entire novel, I do not need to state page numbers.) When you paraphrase, you use your own words, but the length is about the same as the original. (Don't worry—I'm not going to paraphrase *Gone Girl*. You'll have to read that one for yourself, which I highly recommend.)

The Publication Manual (APA, 2010) does not require you to supply a page or paragraph number, but it does encourage the writer to do so (p. 171). I am going to encourage you to list one, and I am going to do so in the examples listed in this section. There is one main reason for this: I think it's best to let your readers know exactly where to find the information for themselves. Will the readers bother to do so? It depends on the essay and why readers might want to look further into the information.

At some point, you may want to write more about your subject. This will help you find the information again quickly as well. If I told you that pages were not required, but I didn't give you a page number, you would have to look through an almost three hundred-page book in order to find one short passage. Do you want your reader to have to do that? Telling the reader exactly where to find the information you are summarizing or paraphrasing is easier and better for everyone. As an instructor, I can tell you that I have rarely tried to look up a student's primary sources. However, on occasion and for different reasons, I will. And so I teach my students to add page or paragraph numbers.

The author-date rules apply to summaries and paraphrasing in the same way that they do for quotes (both long and short.) You can use this decision tree to help you set up your in-text citations. Note how similar they are to quotes. Remember to use the author (year) and add the paragraph or page number to the end (p. 5).

Here is the tree:

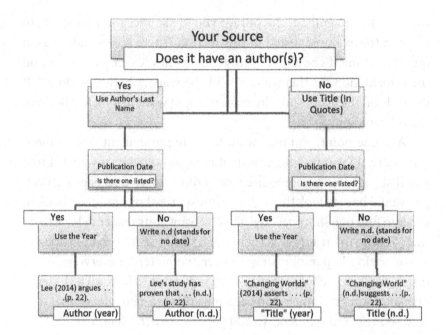

If you have more than one author, the general rule is to use the word *and* in the text and an ampersand in the parenthesis ("In-Text Citations: Author/Authors," 2014, para. 2). The ampersand is this fun little sign: &. Here's an example:

- o Two authors in the text: Lee and Brown (2014)
- o Two authors at the end of the citation: (Lee & Brown, 2014, p. 8)
- o Three authors in the text: Lee, Brown, and White (2014)
- o Three authors at the end of the citation: (Lee, Brown & White, 2014, pp. 6–8)

Let's look at some example of in-text citations of summaries:

SUMMARY OF A PASSAGE WITH AN AUTHOR AND PAGE NUMBER

The prologue of *Something Wicked This Way Comes* sets an eerie stage when it tells the reader that Halloween has come at 3:00 a.m. on October 24. James Nightshade and William Halloway were almost fourteen years old (Bradbury, 1962, p. 1).

SUMMARY OF A PASSAGE WITH AN AUTHOR AND PARAGRAPH NUMBER

A custom oral appliance for those with sleep apnea is an alternative to the CPAP machine, which nearly half of users discontinue. Your dentist takes a mold of your teeth and can later adjust it. Your insurance might also pay for some of the expense (Krieger, 2014, paras. 3–5).

SUMMARY OF A PASSAGE WITH NO AUTHOR AND WITH A PARAGRAPH NUMBER

Because people can fall asleep against their will, narcolepsy can interrupt everyday pursuits such as eating and driving. Major symptoms, including paralysis and loss of voluntary muscle tone can occur before falling asleep ("Narcolepsy Fact Sheet," 2014, para. 2).

SUMMARY OF A PASSAGE WITHOUT AN AUTHOR OR DATE

At eighteen years old in 1792, Johnny left home and moved from Pennsylvania to Ohio to Indiana. In his journal, he planted free seeds from cider mills that he stored in his leather pouch. This is how he became known as "Johnny Appleseed" ("Story of Johnny Appleseed," n. d., paras. 2–4).

EXAMPLES OF A PARAPHRASE

PARAPHRASE OF A PASSAGE WITH AN AUTHOR AND A PARAGRAPH NUMBER

According to Krieger, almost half of CPAP users discontinue them when prescribed for sleep apnea. An alternative to using a CPAP is a custom oral appliance that is worn during sleeping hours. The device forces the jaw forward, opening your airway passage and allowing you to breathe normally. Your dentist simply takes a mold of your teeth and then can customize it when it's returned from the manufacturer. And the good news is that your insurance company might cover some or all of the expense (2014, paras. 3–5).

PARAPHRASE OF A PASSAGE WITH NO AUTHOR AND A PARAGRAPH NUMBER

Employers must accommodate all employees with disabilities, according to the Americans with Disabilities Act. Employers can made concessions like changing work schedules for employees with narcolepsy, so the employee can take a break. In addition, schools must also make accommodations for children and adolescents during school hours ("Narcolepsy Fact Sheet," 2014, para. 37).

PARAPHRASE OF PASSAGE WITHOUT AN AUTHOR OR DATE

In 1792, at the age of eighteen, a man named John and his brother Nathaniel left home. Later, John left his brother and moved from Pennsylvania to the Ohio Valley and later to Indiana. He planted apple seeds each year before he moved further west.

He received his apple seeds free from cider mills he visited and stored them in his leather pouch. While legend has him planting the seeds along waterways and roads, studies have revealed that it's more likely he planted them in nurseries that he created in good spots for planting. Later, he became known as the legendary Johnny Appleseed ("Story of Johnny Appleseed," n. d., paras. 2–3).

A PARAPHRASE WITH THREE AUTHORS IN THE TEXT

Roen, Glau, and Maid discuss the differences between the author's tone and voice. The tone refers to the author's attitude toward his or her work. From the tone, you know what type of essay you are reading. The essay's voice reflects the author's persona (2011, p. 6).

THREE AUTHORS AT THE END OF THE PARAPHRASE

There is a difference between the author's tone and voice. The tone refers to the author's attitude toward his or her work. From the tone, you know what type of essay you are reading. The voice of the student essay reflects the author's persona (Roen, Glau & Maid, 2011, p. 6).

Let's review the general author-date method for in-text citations. Remember, you use them in this order:

- author (or title)
- year (or n. d.)
- page number (or paragraph number)

Use this decision tree to help you set up your in-text citations. There are formatting differences between quotes and summaries/paraphrases (and bigger differences in the long quote), which we discussed in this chapter. Remember that all of the information will be cited in the same order throughout your research paper. It will always be author/title first, followed by the year.

For quotations, a page number or paragraph number is always required. The *Publication Manual* (APA, 2010) only suggests that you use a page number or a paragraph number for summaries and paraphrases. I treat them all the same and will show examples with page or paragraph numbers. This shows consistency and is a good habit to get into for doing research and writing your essays (p. 171).

THE AUTHOR-DATE IN-TEXT CITATION FORMAT DECISION TREE ~~~

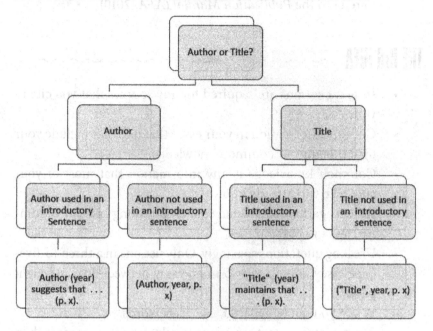

Just a few more notes:

- The date is always the year.
- If you don't know the date, use n. d. (no date).
- If the title is a book or journal, use italics.
- For the title of an article, use quotation marks.
- If there are two authors, use one of these two formats:

  o Lee and Brown (2014) suggest …
  o (Lee & Brown, 2014, p. 5)

- If there are three authors, use one of these two formats:

  o Lee, Brown, and White (2014) suggest that …
  o (Lee, Brown & White, 2014, p. 5)

- If there are more than three authors, you probably are ready to refer to the *Publication Manual (APA,* 2010).

THE BIG IDEA

- In-text citations are required for any sources that you cite in your essay.
- Cite any information in your essay that does not include your own thoughts or common knowledge.
- Common knowledge is any information that most of your audience will already know.
- In-text citations will include quotations (long and short), summaries, and paraphrases.
- Use long quotations sparingly. Only use one in a three-to-five-page essay and up to two in an essay between five and eight pages.
- When you quote material, use exact words.
- Short quotes are forty words or less; long quotes are more than forty words.
- For short quotes, use quotation marks around the words you use from another source.
- Use the block method for formatting long quotes.
- Use an introductory sentence or two to frame your quote. Why are you telling your reader this quote?
- Summaries and quotes are treated the same when formatting.
- All in-text citations use the author-date format. This means you will tell the reader the author followed by the date in parenthesis.
- Quotations require a page number in addition to the author and date.
- Page numbers (or paragraph numbers) are only required for quotations in an APA Style essay. However, it is recommended that you also use them in summaries and paraphrases.
- If you do not know the author, use the title.

- If you do not know the year of publication, use n. d. (no date).
- If you do not know a page number, tell the reader the paragraph number.
- Page number is p. x for one page and pp. X–Y for multiple pages.
- Paraphrase number is para. 1 for one paragraph and paras. 4–5 for multiple paragraphs.
- Never, ever, ever, ever use a website in your in-text citation. If you do not have a title or an author, you probably should not use the source in your essay.

CHAPTER 5

The References Page

Your reference list should appear at the end of your paper. It provides the information necessary for a reader to locate and retrieve any source you cite in the body of the paper. Each source you cite in the paper must appear in your reference list; likewise, each entry in the reference list must be cited in your text. ("References List: Basic Rules", 2014, para. 1)

THE FUNDAMENTALS

- For every in-text citation, there needs to also be a citation in the References page.
- The in-text citation "points" to the References page.
- The References page contains the following information (as much as is available):

  o author
  o title of journal, magazine, or newspaper
  o title of article
  o date of publication (including month, date, and year)

- o page or paragraph number
- o city and state of publication and publishing house
- o DOI number or web address

- Never use *only* a website as a reference entry. It will not meet APA Style formatting if you do use only a website.
- Formatting is as important as the rest of the essay. Double-space the References page throughout.
- Alphabetize the References page by author or title (if there is no author.)
- Don't add any sources that you do not cite in your essay.
- Unlike in the in-text citations, an ampersand should be used. The ampersand is a symbol meaning *and* that looks like this: &. Here is an example Author, A. & Author, B.
- Do not use quotation marks around the titles of journal articles, magazine articles, book chapters, etc.
- Always italicize the title of a book, journal, newspaper, or magazine.
- There is no need to underline websites or use blue print in an essay that will be printed. The 6th edition of *APA Publication Manual* does not refer to whether you should hyperlink whether your References page will be printed or posted online. For the sake of this book, I have chosen not to underline the hyperlinks.

This chapter will show how to format the most common types of sources:

- book (both hard copy and online versions)
- chapters in a book or anthology (both hard copy and online versions)
- articles (journal, magazine, or newspaper)
- websites that contain articles from reliable sources

Since this is a beginners' manual, there isn't much need to look into the other types of sources. It's unlikely you will be using other types of sources in your first research essays. As an instructor, I don't often see sources from places other than these three types of sources in my beginning classes. Once you find yourself in a higher-level course and have a much better understanding of the citation process, you can use the APA's *Publication Manual* to find the details you need for citations from other types of sources.

FORMAT

Remember these rules when formatting your References page ("Reference List," 2014, paras. 3–14):

- With the rest of the essay, the References page should be double-spaced.
- At the top of the page, type "References" and center it.
- Each of your entries should be alphabetized.
- The first line of each entry starts at one inch. Any subsequent lines in that entry should have half-inch tabs (*hanging indentation*).
- All book and journal titles should be italicized.
- Unlike titles of articles that are used in quotes in the body of the essay, they are not put in quotes on the References page.
- Capitalize all main words in the title of the journal, magazine, or newspaper article.
- Capitalize only the following in the title of a book, article, journal, or website:

  o   the first word
  o   the first word after a colon (or dash)
  o   proper nouns

This chapter is broken up to look closely at the main types of documents you will need to source:

- books (print and electronic)
- chapters in a book
- articles from journals, newspapers, magazines (both in print and online), and websites (both with and without authors)

DOI NUMBER

Imagine using a web address link to a journal article you used for a source in your most recent research essay. Now, you want to write another essay using the same source—but the link no longer works. What now? The link can stop working for a multitude of reasons: you have no access to the elibrary you used, the article was updated by another author and no longer exists, or even the website is now defunct. Journals are prohibitively expensive to produce, print, and send out. Most journals are already available online, and the trend is to do so exclusively.

To consolidate the online publishing industry, the DOI number was invented in 1997. Since then, more than 98 million DOI numbers have been assigned to online content ("DOI Handbook," 2014, paras. 5–8). The DOI number is basically a fingerprint for online journals. It is similar to an ISBN number for books in that it is unique to the journal. In fact, some publishers have begun to use the ISBN and have transferred it to a DOI number. This is referred to as the ISBN-A ("Factsheet," 2012, paras. 5–8).

Not all journals have been assigned a DOI number, but as of 2014, more than 98 million DOI numbers have been assigned to journals ("Frequently Asked Questions," 2014, para. 6). There's recently been a new movement to assign DOI numbers to books. I will cover book and journal entries with DOI numbers in your References page.

If your journal or article has been assigned a DOI number, you can find it in one of these places:

- near the copyright notice, generally on the first page of the electronic journal
- in the table of contents, under the title of the article and page number
- on the database landing page ("What is a DOI?," 2014, para. 3)

Here is an example of how to find the DOI in the table of contents. In this example, it is an article in the *New Theater Quarterly*:

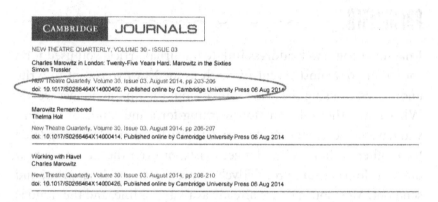

I hope you notice the pattern of the author-date relationship format. You will almost always use an author or author's name first, with very few exceptions. The exceptions are:

- References Page: Author-Date Method
- Author, A. (Year)
- No Author? Use the Title
- "Title of article" (Year)
- An entry from a reference book, such as a dictionary definition
- A book that has an association that is the author. This includes books that have too many authors and contributors that it's impossible to name them all. Since they are attached to a group or association, the association or group is regarded as the author.

- There's an editor or editors. There are many cases where an editor or editors are cited on the cover of a book, particularly in an anthology.

PRINTED BOOKS

If the book was entirely written by one (or more) authors, you will use this section for citing it. If the book is an anthology or has chapters written by various authors, you will want to cite your citation as a chapter.

The way in which the printed book is cited has not changed much in the history of APA citations. That's because the basic information hasn't changed. In its most simple format, it will look like this:

Author, A. (Year). *Title of book*. City, ST: Publisher.

However, there are some slight variations in books that will make you have to change, add, or subtract some of this information.

Tips to remember when citing a book:

- Italicize the title of the book.
- Capitalize only the first letter of the title, unless there is a proper noun in the title.
- Use the author-date format. You will always state the author's name first (or editor), followed by the year of publication for a citation from a book.
- Unlike in the in-text citations, you use an ampersand (&) to denote more than one author or editor: Author, A. & Author, B.

Here is a decision tree that will help you format your References page citations that come from a printed book (*APA*, 2010, pp. 202–203).

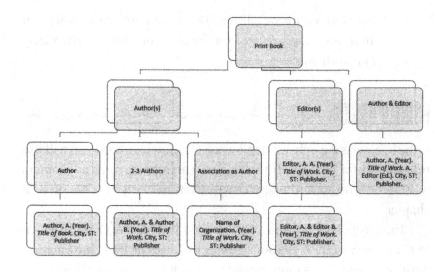

As you can see, in every instance in a printed book, there is an author or editor to begin the entry. There is one exception to the rule where you will not have an author: the printed dictionary. It's unlikely you will ever use a printed dictionary when online dictionaries are so readily available. However, if you do, here is the format ("Cite a Reference to a Book," 2010.) This is how you format a dictionary entry from a print copy:

Title of dictionary (X ed.). (Year). City, ST: Publisher.
Merriam-Webster's collegiate dictionary (11th ed.). (2003). Springfield,
    MA: Merriam-Webster.

PRINT BOOK EXAMPLES

ONE AUTHOR

Bradbury, Ray. (1962). *Something wicked this way comes.* New York,
    NY: Simon and Schuster.

TWO AUTHORS

Johnson-Sheehan, R., & Paine, C. (2013). *Writing today* (2nd ed.). Township, NJ: Pearson.

THREE TO SIX AUTHORS

Roen, D., Glau, G., & Maid, B. (2011). *The McGraw-Hill guide* (2nd Ed.). New York, NY: McGraw-Hill.

ASSOCIATION AS AUTHOR

Modern Language Association. *MLA Handbook for Writers of Research Papers* (7th Ed.). New York, NY: MLA.

EDITOR

Casill, R. V. (Ed.). (1995). *The Norton anthology of short fiction* (5th Ed.). New York, NY: W.W. Norton and Company.

TWO EDITORS

Savage, G., & Sullivan, D. (Eds.). (2001). *Writing a professional life: Stories of technical communicators on and off the job*. Needham Heights, MA: Ally and Bacon.

ONE EDITOR, ONE AUTHOR

Bishop, E. (1995). *One art: Letters*. Giroux, R. (Ed.). New York, NY: Noonday Press.

ONE AUTHOR, TWO EDITORS

Shakespeare, W. (2006, March 2006). *Hamlet. Arden Shakespeare:*
   Third series. Taylor, N., & Thompson, A. (Eds.). New York, NY:
   Bloomsbury Publishing.

ONE AUTHOR AND TWO EDITORS

Shakespeare, W. (2009). *Much ado about nothing (Modern Library*
   Classics). Bate, J., & Rasmussen, E. (Eds.). New York, NY: Random
   House Publishing House, Inc.

TWO AUTHORS, TWO EDITORS

Kerouac, J., & Ginsberg, A. (2010). *Jack Kerouac and Allen Ginsberg:*
   The letters (1st ed.). Morgan, B., & Stanford, D. (Eds.). New York,
   NY: Penguin Group.

E-BOOK

The e-book refers to any book in an electronic format, such as a Kindle
(or other e-book) or a book that's downloaded from a website. Just as
in the print book, if the writer wrote the entire book, you will cite the
entire book. If it's a chapter or article in a book, you can refer to that
section later in this chapter.

   As with a printed book, your book should always have an author
or editor. The exception is a manual or reference book from a reliable source. (For instance, the *Publication Manual of the American
Psychological Association* lists no author because it is authored by a
group of experts. However, we know that it is a reliable source.)

   You'll notice that none of these examples—and none of the examples in any reference entry example—has a "retrieved-on" date. Some
sources will suggest you post the date you retrieved the information.
However, the general rule, according to David Becker (2014) that you

only need to cite the date you retrieved the information if the information is likely to change over time. You should only need to cite wiki sources (or other sources like wikis, where the information changes regularly and without notice) (paras 1–3). As of this writing, wikis are written anonymously (although some are gaining more respect with bylines) and are not considered reliable sources in most educational circles. In fact, I do not allow (and take points off for) any student to use any wiki at any time in the course of a research essay. This book will only discuss reliable sources. A reliable source will not change much over the course of time; therefore, you will not need to use a "retrieved-on" date when you cite your References pages.

TIPS FOR CITING YOUR BOOK ON THE REFERENCES PAGE

- All e-books follow the same format, which is generally the same as the printed format.
- Like the printed book, you will use the author-date format.
- You only capitalize the first word in the title, unless there is a proper noun.
- Italicize the title of all books.
- If the e-book can be retrieved from a website or has a DOI number, add those at the end (after the rest of the citation).
- If you don't have a "type format" (a Kindle Book, for instance) you can delete that information.
- Use an ampersand (&) to denote more than one author or editor: Author, A. & Author, B.
- If you cannot download an e-book, but can find it online, you should use "Available from http://www.yyy123.com" rather than "Retrieved from http://www.yyy123.com" (Paiz, et. All, 2014, para. 15).
- If you cite a Kindle book without a DOI attached, you do not need to use the entire URL in the references. You only need to cite the following: Retrieved from Amazon.com (Lee, 2009).

IN-TEXT CITATIONS E-BOOK DECISION TREE

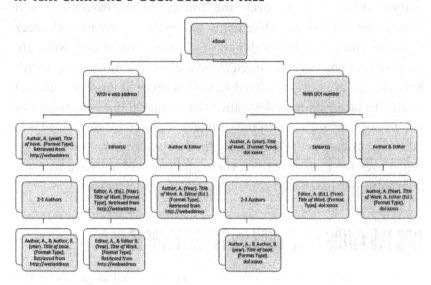

E-BOOK EXAMPLES

E-BOOK WITH A WEB ADDRESS

ONE AUTHOR

Keene, M. (2011). *A practical wedding: Creative ideas for planning a beautiful, affordable, and meaningful celebration.* [e-book format]. Accessed from http://www.indiebound.org/book/9780738215150

TWO AUTHORS

Poe, E. A., & Dickinson, E. (2010). *Poems to scare kids!* [Kindle version]. Retrieved from Amazon.com

THREE AUTHORS

Militello, M., Rallis, S., & Goldring, E. (2009). *Leading with inquiry and action: How principals improve teaching and learning.* Retrieved from eBooks.com

ONE EDITOR

Chaucer, G. (2012). *Chaucer: The complete poetical works.* [Kindle DX version]. W. Skeat (Ed.). Retrieved from Amazon.com

TWO EDITORS

Asante, M., Miike, Y., & Yin, J. (Eds.). (2013). *The global intercultural communication reader* (2nd Ed.). [Kindle version.] Retrieved from Amazon.com

THREE EDITORS

Schneider, F., Gruman, J., & Coutts, L. (Eds.). (2009). *Applied social psychology: Understanding and addressing social and practical problems.* Retrieved from http://books.google.com/books/about/Applied_Social_Psychology.html?id=PG2sIC

ONE AUTHOR, ONE EDITOR

Twain, M. (2014). *Mark Twain on common sense: Timeless advice and words of wisdom from America's most-revered humorist.* S. Brennan (Ed.). Retrieved from Amazon.com

ONE AUTHOR, TWO EDITORS

Shakespeare, W. (2009). *King Lear.* J. Bate & E. Rasmussen (Eds.). [Kindle version]. Retrieved from Amazon.com

TWO AUTHORS, ONE EDITOR

Mayhew, A. & Skeat, W. (2011). *A concise dictionary of Middle English from AD 1150 to 1580* [Kindle version]. J. Brenden (Ed.). Retrieved from Amazon.com

TWO AUTHORS, TWO EDITORS

Kerouac, J., & Ginsberg, A. (2010). *Jack Kerouac and Allen Ginsberg: The letters*. B. Morgan & D. Standford, D. (Eds.). Retrieved from Amazon.com

E-BOOK WITH A DOI NUMBER

ONE AUTHOR

Wenzel, C. (2008). *An introduction to Kant's aesthetics: Core concepts and problems.* doi:10.1002/9780470776599

TWO AUTHORS

Preziosi, D., & Farago, C. (2012). *Art is not what you think it is.* doi:10.1002/9781444354300

THREE AUTHORS

Everitt, B., Landau, S., Leese, M., & Stahl, D. (2011). *Cluster analysis* (5th ed.). doi:10.1002/9780470977811

ONE EDITOR

Beaumont, M. (Ed.). (2008). *Adventures in realism.* doi:10.1002/9780470692035

TWO EDITORS

Arnold, D., & Corbett, D. (Eds.). (2013). *A companion to British art: 1600 to present.* doi:10.1002/9781118313756

THREE EDITORS

Hoaglin, D., Mosteller, F., & Tukey, J. (Eds.). (2011). *Exploring data tables, trends, and shapes.* doi:10.1002/9781118150702

AUTHOR AND EDITOR

Stuart, B. (2013.). *Forensic analytical techniques.* Ando, D. (Ed.). doi:10.1002/9781118496879

CHAPTER IN A BOOK

Sometimes the material you are citing will be a chapter in a book, such as an anthology. If that's the case, the citations are different than if you were quoting from a book with only one author. An anthology or book with an editor listed on the cover means that you are only citing one of the authors in the book—not the entire text.

TIPS FOR CITING CHAPTERS IN YOUR REFERENCES PAGE

- Capitalize the first letter of the title of the chapter and book, unless there is a proper noun in the title.
- Don't use quotations around the title of the chapter. You only need to do that for in-text citations.
- Italicize the title of the book/anthology, but not the title of the chapter.
- If one is assigned, always enter the DOI number at the end of the entry. If no DOI number is available, you can add the web address instead.

- An ampersand (&) is used to denote more than one author or editor: Author, A., & Author, B (APA, 2010, pp. 202–3).

IN-TEXT CITATION BOOK CHAPTER DECISION TREE

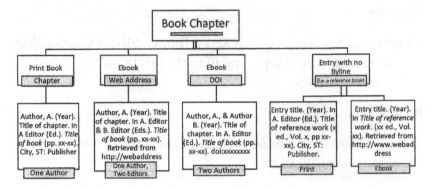

CHAPTER IN A BOOK

PRINT BOOK

ONE AUTHOR, ONE EDITOR

Dario, R. (1997). The death of the empress of China. In Echevarria, R. (Ed.), *Oxford book of Latin American short stories* (pp. 105–110). New York, NY: Oxford Press.

ONE AUTHOR, TWO EDITORS

Hoeniges, C. (2001). It's not Mark Twain's river anymore. In G. Savage & D. Sullivan (Eds.), *Writing a professional life: Stories of technical communicators on and off the job.* Needham Heights, MA: Allyn and Bacon.

ONE AUTHOR, THREE EDITORS

Wedin, R. (2008). Breaking down the barriers. In C. Davis, M. Senechal, & J. Zwicky (Eds.), *The shape of content: Creative writing in mathematics and science* (pp. 174–184). Wellesley, MA: AK Peters, Ltd.

TWO AUTHORS, TWO EDITORS

Cuklanz, L., & Moorti, S. (2011). Television's "new" feminism: Prime-time representations of women and victimization. In G. Dines & J. Humez (Eds.), *Gender, Race, and Class in Media: A critical reader* (pp. 115–127). Thousand Oaks, CA: SAGE Publications.

TWO AUTHORS, THREE EDITORS

Johns, E., & Lovell, M. (2011). Neuropsychological assessment. In J. Silver, T. McAllister, & S. Yudofsky (Eds.), *Traumatic brain injury* (2nd edition) (pp. 127–144). Arlington, VA: American Psychiatric Publishing.

THREE AUTHORS, THREE EDITORS

Arciniegas, D., Anderson, C., & Rojas, D. (2011). Electrophysiological assessment. In J. Silver, T. McAllister, & S. Yudofsky, *Traumatic brain injury* (2nd edition) (pp.), Arlington, VA: American Psychiatric Publishing.

ONE AUTHOR AND ONE EDITOR WITH TWO DIFFERENT PUBLICATION DATES

Poe, E. A. (1995). The Purloined Letter. In R. V. Cassill (Ed.), *The Norton anthology of short fiction* (pp. 1389–1404). New York, NY: W.W. Norton and Company. (Original work published 1845)

CHAPTER IN AN E-BOOK—WEB ADDRESS ~~~~~~~~~~~~~~~~~

ONE AUTHOR, ONE EDITOR

Niedecker, L. (2007). Lake Superior. In N. Baym (Ed.), *The Norton anthology of American literature* (p. 2100). Retrieved from http://books.wwnorton.com/books/detail-contents.aspx?ID=10203

ONE AUTHOR, TWO EDITORS

Dunbar, P. L. (2005). We wear the mask. In D. Stone & S. Young (Eds.), *The anthology: Poems for poetry out loud.* Retrieved from https://archive.org/stream/anthologypoemsfo00ston#page/n3/mode/2up

ONE AUTHOR, THREE EDITORS

Sacks, O. (1993). The bull on the mountain. In R. Silvers, B. Epstein, & R. Hederman (Eds.), *The first anthology: 30 years of New York review of books* (pp. 289–303). Retrieved from https://openlibrary.org/works/OL16028195W/The_first_anthology

TWO AUTHORS, TWO EDITORS

Fink, R., & Gates, R. (2004). Pain assessment. In B. Ferrell & N. Coyle (Eds.), *The textbook of palliative nursing* (pp. 97–130). Retrieved from https://openlibrary.org/books/OL3296502M/Textbook_of_palliative_nursing/daisy

TWO AUTHORS, THREE EDITORS

Stravinsky, I., & Craft, R. (1993). Eau de vie: An interview on Beethoven. In R. Silvers, B. Epstein, & R. Hederman (Eds.), *The first anthology: 30 years of New York review of books* (pp. 103–108).

Retrieved from https://openlibrary.org/works/OL16028195W/ The_first_anthology

ONE AUTHOR, THREE EDITORS

Gilbert, M. (1987). The two footmen. In M. Greenburg, J. Lellenberg, & C. Waugh (Eds.), *The new adventures of Sherlock Holmes: Original stories by eminent mystery writers* (pp. 187–206). Retrieved from https://archive.org/stream/newadventuresofs00vari#page/n3/ mode/2up

CHAPTER IN AN E-BOOK—DOI

ONE AUTHOR, ONE EDITOR

Pelling, C. (2007). Tragedy, rhetoric, and performance culture. In J. Gregory (Ed.), *A companion to Greek tragedy* (pp. 83–102). doi:10.1002/9780470996676.ch6

ONE AUTHOR, TWO EDITORS

Warren, M. L. (2007). Centrarchid identification and natural history. In S. J. Cooke & D.P. Philipp, *Centrarchid fishes: Diversity, biology, and conservation* (pp. 375–481). doi:10.1002/9780470262269.ch13

TWO AUTHORS, ONE EDITOR

Alfonzo, J., & Papavasiliou, N. (2008). Transfer RNA editing enzymes: At the crossroads of affinity and specificity. In H. Smith (Ed.), *RNA and DNA Editing: Molecular mechanisms and their integration into biological systems* (pp. 121–145). doi:10.1002/9780470262269.ch5

TWO AUTHORS, TWO EDITORS

Quinn, S. & Paukert, C. (2007). Centrarchid fisheries. In S. J. Cooke & D.P. Philipp (Eds.), *Centrarchid fishes: Diversity, biology, and conservation* (pp. 312–339). doi:10.1002/9780470262269.ch11

THREE AUTHORS, ONE EDITOR

Zhou, J., Chen, L., & Carmichael, G. (2008). A role for A-to-I editing in gene slicing. In H. Smith (Ed.), *RNA and DNA Editing: Molecular mechanisms and their integration into biological systems* (pp. 190–202). doi:10.1002/9780470262269.ch9

ENTRY WITH NO BYLINE (REFERENCE BOOK)

ONLINE

Plagiarism. (n. d.) In *Merriam-Webster's online dictionary*. Retrieved from http://www.merriam-webster.com/dictionary/plagiarism

PRINT

Abandon. (2001). In *Webster's New World College Dictionary* (4th Ed.). Foster City, CA: IDG Books Worldwide, Inc.

ARTICLE FROM A PERIODICAL

The periodical for this section refers to newspapers, journals, and magazines. However, we will also be discussing how to format a source from a web article, though the formatting is slightly different. When referring to web articles, we are referring only to reliable websites that may or may not have an author, such as WebMD.

Though the basics are the same (author-date format), there are some variations between the three types of articles, particularly between the print and online formats for the journal and magazine. They can include volume and issue numbers. The online web articles may or may not have an author. However, you need to ensure that it comes from a reliable source.

TIPS FOR CITING YOUR ARTICLE ON THE REFERENCES PAGE

- Unlike in the in-text citations, you will not use quotation marks when listing the article title in any reference citation.
- Always italicize the name of the journal, magazine, or newspaper.
- If the magazine or journal does not have a volume or issue number, don't add it.
- Only the first word of the title of the article is capitalized— unless there is a proper noun or following a colon. This is true for all periodicals and articles from websites.
- The title of a periodical is capitalized as it is listed in the original source.
- If one is assigned, always include the DOI number at the end of your entry.
- Use this format for the DOI entry: doi:xx.xxxxxx
- If there is no DOI number and your article is online, you should include the web address at the end of the entry only (and not as a substitute for the entry).
- Use this format for the web entry: Retrieved from http://www.yyyyy.com

This is the general format for the newspaper, journal, or magazine References page entry (APA, 2014, pp. 198–201):

Author, A. (Year). Title of article. *Title of Periodical*, xx, pp.–pp. doi:xx.xxxxxx

Here is a decision tree to help you format your article entry in the reference page:

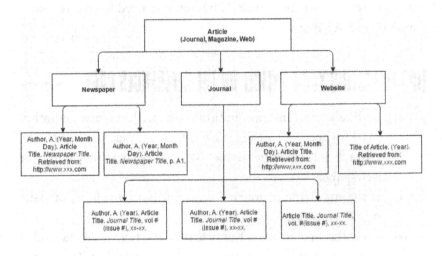

ARTICLE EXAMPLES

NEWSPAPER—PRINT

ONE AUTHOR

Pabst, Georgia. (2014, September 30). Domestic violence claims 39. *The Milwaukee Journal Sentinel*, pp. 1B, 5B.

TWO AUTHORS

Richards, E. & Kissinger, M. (2014, September 30). *The Milwaukee Journal Sentinel*, pp. 1A, 4A.

PRINT—NO AUTHOR

Prayers said for Briton killed by Islamic fighters. (2014, October 5). *The Milwaukee Journal Sentinel*, 3A.

NEWSPAPER—ONLINE

NO AUTHOR

When privacy and law enforcement collide. (2014, September 30). *New York Times.* Retrieved from http://www/nytimes.com

ONE AUTHOR

Eckholm, E. (2014, October 5). California voters to decide on sending fewer criminals to prison. *New York Times.* Retrieved from http://www.nytimes.com

TWO AUTHORS

De La Merced, M. & Isaac, M. (2014, October 6). Yahoo in talks to sink some of its Alibaba cash into Snapchat. *New York Times. Retrieved from http://dealbook.nytimes.com*

JOURNAL—PRINT

ONE AUTHOR

Carkeet, D. (2014). The Twain Shall Meet. *Smithsonian,* 45 (1), 74–90.

TWO AUTHORS

Gioia, D. & Pitre, E. (1990). Multiparadigm perspectives on theory building. *Academy of Management Review,* 15 (4), 584–602.

JOURNAL—DOI

The DOI number might be listed with as a web address link or just as the DOI number. Therefore, the DOI could be cited like one of these two examples:

- doi:xx.xxxxx/xxxxx
- http://dx.doi.org/10.0000/0000

ONE AUTHOR

Aspelmeyer, M. (2009). Quantum tomography: Measured measurement. *Nature Physics*, 5, 11–12. doi:10.1038/nphys1170

Henrich, A. (2011). Reducing Math Anxiety: Findings from Incorporating Service Learning into a Quantitative Reasoning Course at Seattle University. *Numeracy*, 4 (2), 9. http://dx.doi.org/10.5038/1936-4660.4.2.9

TWO AUTHORS

Alvesson, M., & Karreman, D. (2013). The closing of critique, pluralism, and reflexivity: A response to Hardy and Grant and some wider reflections. *Human Relations*, 66 (10), 1353–1371. doi:10.1177/0018726713477460

Latiolais, M. P., & Laurence, W. (2009). Engaging math-avoidant college students. *Numeracy*, 2 (2), 5. http://dx.doi.org/10.5038/1936-4660.2.2.5

THREE AUTHORS

Chia-Huei, W., Parker, S., & de Jong, J. (2014). Need for cognition as an antecedent of individual innovation behavior. *Journal of Management*, 40 (15), 1511–1534. doi:10.1177/0149206311429862

FOUR AUTHORS

El-Dien, N., Zayed, A., Gehad, G., & El-Nahas, G. (2005). Two spectrophotometric assays for dopamine derivatives in pharmaceutical products and in biological samples of schizophrenic patients using copper tetramine complex and tri-iodide reagent. *BioMed Research International*, 2005 (1), 1–9. http://dx.doi.org/10.1155/JBB.2005.1

JOURNAL—ONLINE

ONE AUTHOR

Ball, S., & James, H. (2009). Making law teaching accessible and inclusive. *Journal of Information, Law & Technology (JILT)*, 2009 (3), 34–45. Retrieved from http://go.warwick.ac.uk/jilt/2009_3/ball

TWO AUTHORS

Li, Y., & Zon, G. (1991). NMR and molecular modeling evidence for a GA mismatch base pair in a purine-rich DNA duplex. *PNAS*, 88 (1), 26–30. Retrieved from http://www.pnas.org/content/88/1.toc

THREE AUTHORS

Hongying, F., Qingping, W., & Xiaoxia, K. (2008). Influence of euonymus alatus sied extracts on MDCK proliferation and high concentration of glucose induced cell injury. *Life Science Journal*, 5 (4), 41–46. Retrieved from http://www.lifesciencesite.com/lsj/life0504/

MAGAZINE—PRINT

NO AUTHOR

The Affordable Care Act: A primer. (2014, April). *Healthcare Contracting*, 11 (2), 6–7.

ONE AUTHOR

Marquis, A. L. (2014, Fall). Rallying cry. *National Parks*, 88 (4), 16–18.

TWO AUTHORS

Lutzer, C., & Marengo, J. (2004, February). Extremal curves of a rotating ellipse. *Mathematics Magazine*, 32 (1), 55–61.

MAGAZINE—ONLINE

NO AUTHOR

Happiness is handmade. (2014, December). *American Patchwork and Quilting*, 22 (6), 29–33. Available from http://www.zinio.com/reader.jsp?issue=416317039&e=true

ONE AUTHOR

Weir, K. (2014, October). Translating psychological science. *Monitor*, 45 (9). Retrieved from http://www.apa.org/monitor/2014/10/index.aspx

TWO AUTHORS

Harris, W., & Webb, J. (2014, July). Life inside a globular cluster. *Astronomy*, 42 (7), 18–23. Available from http://www.zinio.com/reader.jsp?issue=416304404&e=true

WEB ARTICLE

NO AUTHOR

What is MLA style? (2014). Retrieved August 5, 2014, from http://www.mla.org/style

ONE AUTHOR

Preidt, Robert. (2014, April 17). Bacteria in contact lens solution. Retrieved from http://www.webmd.com/eye-health/news/20140417/bacteria-may-survive-longer-in-contact-lens-solution-than-thought

ORGANIZATION AS AUTHOR

American Heart Association. (2014, September 10). Understanding your risk for cardiac arrest. Retrieved from http://www.heart.org/HEARTORG/Conditions/More/CardiacArrest/Understand-Your-Risk-for-Cardiac-Arrest_UCM_307909_Article.jsp

PDF DOCUMENT

Merkely, G., & Allen, R. Center Pivot Uniformity Evaluation [PDF document]. Retrieved from http://ocw.usu.edu/Biological_and_Irrigation_Engineering/Sprinkle___Trickle_Irrigation/6110__L14_Center_Pivot_Uniformity_Evaluation.pdf

PODCAST

Lindsay, P. (2016, August 1). Up and vanished. Retrieved from : http://
itunes.apple.com

ONE PRODUCER

Acevedo, A. (Producer). (2014, October 7). Nerdist writers panel:
Manhattan [161]. *Nerdist*. Retrieved from http://www.nerdist.
com/pepisode/nerdist-writers-panel-161-manhattan-creator-
sam-shaw/

TWO PRODUCERS

Cole, S., & Calhoun, B. (Producers). (2014). A not-so-simple majority
[534]. This American Life from WBEZ. Retrieved from http://
www.thisamericanlife.org/radio-archives/episode/534/a-not-so-s
imple-majority

NOTE ON THE USE OF WEBSITES IN REFERENCES PAGE

Notice that the only time a website is posted is at the end of the reference citation. There are no citations that include only the web address
in the in-text citations or on the References page. The purpose for
posting the web address is solely to be able to quickly find the source.
That's it. It is not a citation in and of itself. This is really important,
because your instructor or professor could potentially take off points
if you don't cite your sources properly on the References page.

Depending on the type of essay, you can lose more points. For
instance, if you are turning in an eight-page research paper that you
had four weeks to work on, you want to make sure that it is properly
cited. Using only websites as your citations—both in text and in the
References page—will earn you a much lower grade. It's really important to get your citations properly cited and to try to understand

how they are organized. Once you do, you will find it much easier to cite your sources easily. You might not get them correct every time, but as long as you show some effort, your instructor or professor will understand—and you will improve over time.

There is a quick reference guide for both in-text citations and the References page in the "Special Features" section of this book. Once you get a feel for how to format your in-text citations and the References page using the author-date method, you can use that section to format either your in-text citations or your References page.

THE BIG IDEA

- The References citation entries are longer versions of the now-familiar author-date format.
- Double-space the References page throughout.
- Put References in middle justified on top.
- If you cite a source in the text, you must add an entry on your reference page.
- The in-text citation "points" to the References page.
- The References page contains the following information (as much as is available):

  o author
  o title of article
  o title of journal, newspaper, or magazine
  o date of publication (including month, date and year)
  o page or paragraph number
  o city of publication and publishing house
  o web address or DOI number

- The entry on your References page must refer directly from the in-text citation.

- If your in-text citation is (Lee, 2014, p. 6), then your citation will be: Lee, B. (2014). *Title of book*. New York, NY: Lee Publications.
- If your in-text citation is ("The Way We Were," 2010, p. 78), then your citation will be: The way we were. (2010). Retrieved from http://www.yyyyyyy.com
- *Never* use a website for an in-text citation. APA Style follows the author-date format. If you do not have an author or name of an article, you should not use the source.
- The only time you put a web address in an entry on the References page is after the entry, per the guidelines. Your References page should not solely list web addresses as your sources.
- The References page also uses the author-date format. If there is no author, you will use the name of the editor. If there is no editor, use the title of your article.
- You will add a web address at the end of your citation if:

  o the source was retrieved online
  o the online source does not have a DOI number
  o if you cannot download an e-book, but can find it on-line, you should use "Available from http://www.yyyyy. com" rather than "Retrieved from http://www.yyyyy.com" (Paiz, et. All, 2014, para. 15)
  o denote more than one author or editor: Author, A. & Author, B.

- Capitalize the first letter of the title of the chapter and book, unless there is a proper noun in the title.
- Quotations are not used to note the title of the chapter. The reader will know this is the title of an article because the title of the book, magazine, journal, or newspaper is italicized.

- Enter the DOI number at the end of the entry, if one is assigned. If no DOI number is available, use the web address instead.
- Only the first word of the title of the article or book is capitalized unless there is a proper noun or following a colon.
- Use capitalization in full for the title of journals, magazines, and newspapers.

CHAPTER 6

Rules of Mechanics

Writing in APA is more than simply learning the formula for citations or following a certain page layout. APA also includes the stylistics of your writing, from point of view to word choice. (Paiz, et al., 2013, para. 1)

THE FUNDAMENTALS

- APA Style formatting has rules regarding clarity, conciseness, and grammar.
- The rules will be referred to in general as the *rules of mechanics* or mechanics.
- The mechanics should be used in all APA Style-formatted essays, whether there is any research and citation in the essay or not.

In the first chapter, we learned about formatting APA Style essays. You do not need to have a research essay in order to format your essay in APA Style. There are some other elements that you should consider when writing your essay that aren't a part of the research or citation process—but are a big part of the writing process.

For the purposes of this chapter and APA Style, we will refer to mechanics as an umbrella term that will cover all sections of this chapter, including clarity, conciseness, voice, tone, and any grammar and punctuation. A similar term that could also be used is *stylistics*, but I felt that would be too confusing to refer to stylistics and APA Style. The *APA Publication Manual* refers to punctuation, spelling, capitalization, italics, abbreviations, numbers, metrication, statistical and mathematical copy, and equations as the "mechanics of style." I don't want to confuse you, so I'm just going to simply call it mechanics. However, I am also including some other elements such as voice, clarity, grammar, organization, and reducing bias in the term.

The point of this book is not to discuss the writing composition. However, there are elements of the writing process that need to be included when writing your essay in APA Style. Since this is a beginner book, this chapter will not cover every single element. APA's *Publication Manual* spends nearly sixty-five pages to the discussion of these elements. Because APA Style is also used by academic scholars who are presenting their written research, not all of the mechanics need to be covered in this book. We will cover the main points and the ones that you will likely need to know as you prepare your essay.

Those sections will include:

- voice (point of view)
- conciseness and clarity
- bias reduction
- grammar and usage
- spelling
- capitalization
- italics
- abbreviations
- punctuation

VOICE/POINT OF VIEW

You've likely studied the three different points of view in writing: first person ("I" voice), second person ("you" voice), and third person ("we" voice). All APA Style essays and work should be in first person (Paiz, et. al., 2014, paras. 1–4).

INSTEAD OF THIS:

At the corner of Hickory and First Streets, they should put a stop sign.

STATE THIS:

I recommend that a stop sign be placed at the corner of Hickory and First Streets.

OR EVEN THIS:

A stop sign should be placed at the corner of Hickory and First Streets.

In the last statement, the "I" is inferred, meaning the reader will know by reading this that it is your opinion that a stop sign should be posted at the corner of Hickory and First Streets.

First person is recommended because it resolves the issue of using a passive voice, and it also makes the essay more clear and concise.

CLARITY AND CONCISENESS (WORDINESS)

In beginner writing and other classes where you will be using APA Style, paper lengths are set to avoid being arbitrary. While many students new to writing papers or research essays that are three to five pages long or five to eight pages long might find it difficult, it's important to be as clear and concise as possible in your writing. This means that you should avoid wordiness in your writing. Purdue's OWL (2014) also recommends that you avoid "poetic language" such as using metaphors and figurative language in your writing (Paiz, et al. (2014) para. 18). Of course, you can't avoid using metaphors in some English or literature essays. However, it's unlikely you would be using APA Style for an English or literature class.

How do you avoid wordiness and ensure that your writing is concise? According to Purdue's OWL (2013), there are three general rules for ensuring your writing is concise (Weber and Hurm, 2013, Paras. 1–22):

- Replace vague and confusing words and terms with specific words and phrases.
- Example of a wordy sentence: I need to remove wordiness from my sentences by removing words that might be repetitive so that my essays are more clearly stated.
- Example of that sentence in more concise terms: I removed redundant words for clarity from my essay.
- Read every sentence on its own and ensure that it is unique and important to your paragraph/essay.
- Combine sentences to remove redundancy and repetition.
- Example of two redundant ideas: My instructor says that I should combine sentences to avoid wordiness. So, I need to do that so that my writing might be less wordy and avoid repetitive ideas.
- Combine those sentences for this effect: If I combine sentences, my essay will be less wordy—and I will avoid redundancy.

AUTHOR'S ASIDE

Writing clearly and concisely is extremely important in academic writing. However, it's sometimes hard to fill five or eight pages in an essay, particularly if writing research essays is new to you or if you haven't written a research essay for a long time. Sometimes, when you're having trouble "filling the space," you might find that you are wordy on purpose to meet that page requirement. It's really a terrible habit to get into, and I recommend you spend your time being concise and writing the in-text citations and your References page properly. If you don't, you might find yourself in a rut that you can't get out of.

Writing essays can be a chore—and it can be difficult—but it doesn't have to be. Choose the right topic for the paper length and do enough research so that you can write a strong, academic paper worthy of the class you are taking. Essays will only get more complicated and longer over the course of your academic career. I'm not saying that to scare you because you shouldn't be scared, but you should be prepared and knowledgeable about what you need to be composing. If you have questions, ask your professor to clarify. Don't cut corners. Don't start your academic career with bad habits. This is an education, and you should work to make the most of your academic career!

BIAS REDUCTION

While a discussion of bias reduction (which can refer to gender roles, racial and ethnic identity, sexual orientation, age, and disabilities) is generally needed for reporting the results of research or experiments, it's important to have a discussion about it in this chapter. It's imperative to note that language and preference of terms changes over time. And in the course of your research, you might find you need to describe someone else's research in your own words. This is when it's important to remove any language bias that might occur inadvertently or purposefully. When writing about any of these topics, it's important to remember the following to remove any bias in your writing (*APA*, 2014, pp. 70–77):

- Be specific. If you are discussing an age group, you need only state "ages 40–55."
- Be considerate about labels—and use the labels that are preferred by a specific group. Make an effort to find out what

the group you are writing about prefers or use commonly accepted names, titles, or labels.

Please note that these rules are not rigid; they are simply guidelines to direct your writing. Avoid language bias in your essays, which is different from stating your opinion or arguing a point. In order to make your point or state your opinion clearly, you must be respectful and support your points with research and sound logical argument instead of bias.

GRAMMAR AND USAGE

ACTIVE VERBS

When writing, use active verbs. This ensures that your sentences are active. Active sentences are easier to read and more concise. Much of the time, they are also more interesting. Active verbs describe what the subject of the verb is doing.

HERE IS AN EXAMPLE OF AN ACTIVE SENTENCE:

John runs the dishwasher nightly.

THE PASSIVE EXAMPLE OF THIS SAME SENTENCE WOULD LOOK LIKE THIS:

The dishwasher is run by John nightly.

Do you see the difference? Which is more interesting to read? Which is more concise? The active sentence is. (How much more active can a sentence be than the previous one, right?)

Barnes and Johnson (2014) concede that the results of the survey might be flawed (pp. 45–47).

The results of the survey could be flawed, it has been conceded by Barnes and Johnson (2014, pp. 45–47).

The easiest trick is to make the verb in the sentence only one word (or the fewest number of words possible.) Once you start adding "it has been" or "could be" you are making the sentence passive.

SUBJECT-VERB AGREEMENT

The *Publication Manual* discusses subject-verb agreement, but this is true in general of all grammar. The subject and verb should always "agree." This means simply that the verb in your sentence should be singular if the subject is singular, and it should be plural if the subject is plural (APA, 2010, pp. 78–79.)

Here are some examples:

SINGULAR SUBJECT-SINGULAR VERB

- Penny writes every Wednesday and Thursday.
- The result of the survey was published in the quarterly journal.

PLURAL SUBJECT-PLURAL VERB

- Penny and Byron write every Wednesday and Thursday.
- The results of the survey were published in the quarterly journal.

The quickest method for ensuring subject-verb agreement in your essay is to find only the subject and verb in a sentence and check that they are both singular and plural. For instance:

- Result was
- Results were

When you isolate the subject and the verb, it is much easier to see whether they agree or not. If they don't agree, it is easily remedied!

SPELLING

The Publication Manual (APA, 2010) ascertains that you should only use words that are included in the following dictionaries:

- *Merriam Webster's Collegiate Dictionary (2005)*
- *The APA Dictionary of Psychology (2007)*
- *Webster's Third New International Dictionary (2002)*

If it's not listed in one of these References, then don't use the word. And if there are multiple spellings of a word, use the first spelling listed.

CAPITALIZATION

The *Publication Manual's* (APA, 2010) guidelines are that you should capitalize:

- the first letter in a sentence
- major words in titles and headings
- proper nouns

ITALICS

Although there is a long list in the *Publication Manual* (APA, 2010), most of them refer to scholarly writing. However, for beginners, the most important use of italics is to always, always, always italicize the following titles:

- books
- periodicals (journals, magazines, newspapers, etc.)
- films
- videos
- TV shows
- microfilm publications

There are *no* exceptions to this rule.

ABBREVIATIONS

When citing an organization with a long name, it is acceptable to use an abbreviation after the first instance. As an example, you might use American Psychological Association in the first instance. Following that, you can refer to it as APA, as long as you let the reader know the appropriate abbreviation (APA, 2010).

PUNCTUATION

The APA recommends that you adhere to the following rules (APA, 2010, pp. 87–100):

- Use only one space between all words, including after commas, semicolons, and end marks (periods, exclamation points, question marks, etc.)

- Use a serial comma if it has three or more items. For instance: Adey, Brown, and Cole (2014) argue …
- Use a comma after each author or editor's name in the References page. For instance: Adey, A., & Brown, B.
- Use a comma to set off the year in exact dates. For instance: January 1, 2000, was the beginning of the new millennium.
- Use a comma to set off the year in parenthetical (in-text) citations. For instance: (Cole, 2014).
- Use quotation marks to frame all short quotes (forty words or less).
- Use quotation marks for titles of articles for all in-text citations. For instance: Brown's (2014) article, "The State of Healthcare Today" argues …
- Place the year of publication in parenthesis in in-text citations when you use the author to frame your sentence. For instance: Brown (2014) proposes in his study that …
- Use parenthesis for in-text citations in the author-date format at the end of a sentence. For instance: The study clearly argues for a reduced rate in gas prices (Brown, 2014, p. 16).

THE BIG IDEA

- APA Style refers not just to formatting your in-text citations and the References page. It also refers to grammar and mechanics and clarity and conciseness.
- Refer to the *Merriam-Webster* dictionary to find the correct spelling. If the word is not in the dictionary, don't use it in your essay.
- Ensure subject-verb agreement in each sentence. If the subject is singular, the verb should be singular. If the subject is plural, the verb should also be plural.

FINAL THOUGHTS

Abraham Lincoln said, "Upon the subject of education … I can only say that I view it as the most important subject which we as a people may be engaged in." ("Great Educational Quotes," 2014)

If you learn anything that you need to remember the most after reading this book it is this: author-date method.

That's simple enough, right? That's all the information you need to remember, and you are on your way to properly citing your in-text citations and your References page. Well, mostly. There are a few more things that you should keep in your wheelhouse, just in case.

THE BIGGEST DEAL

- The author-date method is used in the in-text citations in the following way:

  o Author (date) states …
  o (Author, date)
  o The author-date method is used in the References page in the following way:
  o Author, A. (Date). Title.

- You can set up your essay using a title page, double-spacing, and some other formatting guidelines as an APA Style essay, even if you don't use any research in your essay.
- Remember to be as concise as possible, use active language, and ensure that the subject and verb agree. These are all APA Style guidelines, but the subject-verb agreement is a grammar rule you should always follow.
- Never, ever, ever use a website in your in-text citations. Ever. If you don't have an author or title, don't consider the website reliable.
- Never, ever, ever use a website in your References page—except as at the end of the entry (after you put in the author, date title, etc.) as a way for the reader to find the source only.
- Never, ever, ever plagiarize. That's just bad news. Do the work yourself. You owe it to yourself to get the very best out of the education you are paying for. And you never know, you might learn something!

A CLOSER LOOK

~~~~~~~~~~~~~~~~~~~~~~~~~~~~~~~~~~~~~~~

THE REFERENCES PAGE EXAMPLE

REFERENCES

Aspelmeyer, M. (2009). Quantum tomography: Measured measurement. *Nature Physics*, 5, 11–12. doi:10.1038/nphys1170

Ball, S., & James, H. (2009). Making law teaching accessible and inclusive. *Journal of Information, Law & Technology (JILT)*, Retrieved from http://go.warwick.ac.uk/jilt/2009_3/ball

Bradbury, Ray. (2011). *Fahrenheit 541*. [Kindle Fire version]. Retrieved from Amazon.

Bradbury, Ray. (1962). *Something wicked this way comes.* NY: Simon and Schuster.

Casill, R. V. (Ed.). (1995). *The Norton anthology of short fiction (5ᵗʰ ed.).* New York, NY: W.W. Norton and Company.

Plath, S. (2000). *The unabridged journals.* K. V. Kukil (Ed.). New York, NY: Anchor.

Poe, E. A. (1995). Fall of the house of Usher. In R. V. Cassill (Ed.), *The Norton Anthology of Short Fiction* (pp. 1373–1388). New York, NY: W.W. Norton and Company. (Original work published 1839)

Preidt, Robert. (2014, April 17). Bacteria in Contact Lens Solution. Retrieved from http://www.webmd.com/eye-health/news/20140417/bacteria-may-survive-longer-in-contact-lens-solution-than-thought

Trussler, S. (2014, August 6). Charles Marowitz in London: Twenty-five years hard: Marowitz in the Sixties. *New Theatre Quarterly*, 30 (3), 203-206. doi:10.1017/S0266464X14000402

What is MLA Style? (2014). Retrieved from http://www.mla.org/style

BASIC IN-TEXT CITATION FORMATTING

ONE AUTHOR

Adey (2014) argues ... (p. 167).
(Adey, 2014, p. 167)

TWO AUTHORS

Adey and Brown (2014) maintains ... (p. 167).
(Adey & Brown, 2014, p. 167)

THREE AUTHORS

First instance: Adey, Brown, and Cole (2014) acknowledge that ...
(pp. 88–91).
Second instance: Adey et al. (2014) further argue ... (pp. 88–91).
First instance: (Adey, Brown & Cole, 2014, p. 10)
Subsequent instances: (Adey et al., 2014, p. 10)

ONE EDITOR

Edwards (2014) argues that ... (pp. 12–16).
(Edwards, 2014, pp. 12–16)

TWO EDITORS

Edwards and Bell (2014) propose ... (pp. 12–16).
(Edwards & Bell, 2014, pp. 12–16)

THREE EDITORS

First instance: Edwards, Bell, and Carter (2014) propose ... (pp. 12–16).
Subsequent instances: Edwards et al. (2014) further described ... (p. 15).
First instance: (Edwards, Bell, & Carter, 2014, pp. 12–16)
Subsequent instances: (Edwards et al., 2014, p. 15).

NO AUTHOR

(Use abbreviated title if the title is longer than 5 words)
"Title of article," (2014) reports ... (p. 5).
("Title of article," 2014, p. 5)

ORGANIZATION AS AUTHOR

Harvard University (2014) reports ... (pp. 34–56).
(Harvard University, 2014, pp. 34–56)

ORGANIZATION KNOWN BY ABBREVIATIONS AS AUTHOR

First instance: American Heart Association ([AHA] 2014) found ... (p. 34).
Subsequent instances: AHA (2014) also revealed ... (p. 56).
First instance: (American Heart Association [AHA], 2014, p. 34)
Subsequent instances: (AHA, 2014, p. 34)

QUICK REFERENCE GUIDE TO IN-TEXT CITATIONS AND REFERENCES PAGE ENTRY CITATIONS FOR APA STYLE

This guide is designed as a quick reference for you to easily find examples and proper formatting for in-text citations and the References page citation entry. The organization is as follows:

- generic References page example
- real-world References page example
- in-text citation example
- alternative in-text citation example

Though the *Publication Manual of the American Psychological Association* (APA, 2010) does not require the author to post page or paragraph numbers in every instance, it is recommended. Therefore, all in-text citation examples will include a page or paragraph number(s). (Note that some examples in this textbook have not been double-spaced, for your ease of use. Please be sure to double space all APA Style essays in their entirety.)

PRINT BOOK

AUTHOR

Author, A. (Year). *Title of book*. City, ST: Publisher.
Grisham, J. (2014). *Sycamore row*. New York, NY: Dell Mass Market
　　Edition.

　　Adey (2014) argues that ... (p. 15).
　　(Adey, 2014, p. 15).

TWO AUTHORS

Author, A., & Author, B. (Year). *Title of book*. City, ST: Publisher.
Hacker, D., & Sommers, N. (2012). *A writer's reference for multimodal
　　projects*. Boston, MA: Bedford/St. Martin's.

　　Adey and Brown (2014) propose ... (pp. 145–156).
　　(Adey and Brown, 2014, pp. 145–156)

THREE AUTHORS

Author, A., & Author, B., & Author, C. (Year). *Title of book*. City, ST:
　　Publisher.
Whitman, W., Dickinson, E., & Frost, R. (1996). *Three great American
　　poets*. Ann Arbor, MI: Tally Hall Press.

　　First instance: Adey, Brown, and Cole (2014) acknowledged that ...
　　(pp. 66–89).
　　Second instance: Adey et al. (2014) further argued ... pp. 66–89.
　　First instance: (Adey, Brown, & Cole, 2014, p. 15)
　　Subsequent instances: (Adey et al., 2014, p. 15)

THREE AUTHORS (BOOK WITH AN EDITION)

Author, A., & Author, B., & Author, C. (Year). *Title of book (2nd ed.)*. City, ST: Publisher.

Alred, G., Brusaw, C., & Oliu, W. (2011). *Handbook of technical writing* (10th ed.). Boston, MA: Bedford/St. Martin's.

First instance: Adey, Brown, and Cole (2014) acknowledge that … (pp. 88–91).
Second instance: Adey et al. (2014) further argue … (pp. 88–91).
First instance: (Adey, Brown, & Cole, 2014, p. 10)
Subsequent instances: (Adey et al., 2014, p. 10)

ASSOCIATION AS AUTHOR

Name of Organization. (Year). *Title of publication*. City, ST: Publisher.

National Wildlife Association. (1997). *Wading into wetlands*. New York, NY: McGraw-Hill.

The National Wildlife Association (1997) proposed … (p. 75).
First Citation: (The National Wildlife Association [NWA], 1997, p. 75).
Subsequent citations: (NWA, 1997, p. 75).

TWO AUTHORS, ONE EDITOR

Author, A., & Author, B. (Year). Title of publication. A. Editor (Ed.). City, ST: Publisher.

Browning, R., & Browning, E. B. (2003). *Browning: Poems (everyman's library pocket poets*. P. Washington (Ed.). New York, NY: Everyman's Library.

Adey and Brown (2014) recommend … (pp. 45–56).
(Adey & Brown, 2014, pp. 45–56)

ONE AUTHOR, TWO EDITORS

Author, A. (Year). *Title of book: Subtitle of book.* A. Editor & B. Editor
(Eds.). City, ST: Publishing House.
Frost, R. (1995). Robert Frost: Collected poems, prose, and plays
(Library of America). R.
Poirier & M. Richardson (Eds.). New York, NY: Penguin Putnam Inc.

Adey, A. (1995) argued … (p. 45).
(Adey, 1995, p. 45).

EDITOR

Editor, A. (Ed.). (Year). *Title of book: Subtitle of book.* City, ST:
Publishing House.
Gostin, L. (Ed.). (2002). *Public health law and ethics: A reader.* Berkeley,
CA: University of California Press.

Adey (2014) maintains … (pp. 34–56)
(Adey, 2014, pp. 34–56)

TWO EDITORS

Editor, A., & Editor, B. (Eds.). (Year). *Title of book: Subtitle of book.*
City, ST: Publisher.
Johnson-Eiola, J., & Selber, S. (Eds.). (2004). *Central works in technical
communication.* New York, NY: Oxford University Press.

Adey and Brown (2014) advise … (pp. 59–129).
(Adey & Brown, 2014, pp. 59–129).

ONE AUTHOR, ONE EDITOR

Author, A. (Year). *Title of book.* Editor, A. (Ed.). City, ST: Publishing
House.

Twain, M. (2014). *Mark Twain on common sense: Timeless advice and words of wisdom from America's most-revered humorist.* Brennan, S. (Ed.). New York, NY: Skyhorse Publishing.

Adey (2014) argued … (p. 24).
(Adey, 2014, p. 24)

TWO EDITORS, TWO AUTHORS

Author, A., & Author, B. (Year). *Title of book.* A. Editor, & B. Editor (Eds.) City, ST: Publishing House.
Kerouac, J., & Ginsberg, A. (2010). *Jack Kerouac and Allen Ginsberg: The letters.* B. Morgan, & D. Standford (Eds.). New York, NY: Penguin Group.

Adey and Brown (2014) suggested … (p. 13)
(Adey & Brown, 2014, p. 13)

E-BOOK

All e-books, free e-book downloads, and Kindle versions of e-books always will be denoted with "retrieved from." If you purchased the e-book or if it can be read but not downloaded from a web address, then you would use "available from." Use the full URL address, except for Kindle books, which you just denote "retrieved from Amazon. com." (Paiz et al., 2014, "Electronic Books").

WEB ADDRESS

AUTHOR

Author, A. (Year). *Title of book.* Available from http://www.yyyyy. com/xxxxx

Rabinowitz, A. (2007). *Life in the valley of death: The fight to save tigers in a land of guns, gold, and green.* Available from https://play. google.com/store/books/details/Alan_Rabinowitz_Life_in_the_ Valley_of_Death?_bbid=14877&_bbreg=us&_bbtype=blog&id= qnFID5-2z-kC&PAffiliateID=1l3vnbh

Adey (2014) argues that ... (pp. 123–167).
(Adey, 2014, pp. 123–167)

TWO AUTHORS

Author, A., & Author, B. (Year). *Title of book.* Available from http:// www.yyyyy.com/xxxxx
Frost, R., Dickinson, E., & Poe, E. A. (2010). *Do you ever think as a hearse goes by?* [Kindle version]. Retrieved from Amazon.com

THREE AUTHORS

Author, A., Author, B., & Author, C. (Year). *Title of book.* Available from http://www.yyyyy.com/xxxxx
Whitehead, B., Jensen, D., & Boschee, F. (2013). *Planning for technology: A guide for school administrators, technology coordinators, and curriculum leaders.* Available from http://books.google.com/ books/about/Planning_for_Technology.html?id=KquxS-pz4AQC

Adey and Brown (2014) argue that ... (p. 127).
(Adey & Brown, 2014, p. 127)

EDITOR

Editor, A. (Ed.). (Year). *Title of book.* Available from Http://www. yyyyy.com/xxxxx
Guinan, J. (Ed.). (2009). *The Investopedia guide to wall speak: The terms you need to know to talk like Cramer, think like Soros, and*

buy like Buffett (1ˢᵗ ed.). Available from http://www.abebooks.com/
Investopedia-Guide-Wall-Speak-Terms-Need/12284030962/bd

Edwards (2014) argues that ... (pp. 12–16).
(Edwards, 2014, pp. 12–16)

TWO EDITORS

Editor, A., & Editor, B. (Eds.). (Year). *Title of book*. Available from
http://www.yyyyy.com/xxxxx
Dickson, T., & Gray, T. (2011). *Risk management in the outdoors*.
[Etextbook Digital version]. Available from http://www.cours-
esmart.com/risk-management-in-the-outdoors/tracey-j-dickson-
tonia-l-gray/dp/9781139511865

Edwards and Bell (2014) propose ... (pp. 12–16).
(Edwards & Bell, 2014, pp. 12–16)

THREE EDITORS

Editor, A., Editor, B., & Editor, C. (Eds.). (Year). *Title of book*. Available
from http://www.yyyyy.com/xxxxx
Schneider, F., Gruman, J., & Coutts, L. (Eds.). (2009). *Applied social
psychology: Understanding and addressing social and practical
problems*. Retrieved from http://books.google.com/books/about/
Applied_Social_Psychology.html?=BPG_JE052sIC

First instance: Edwards, Bell, and Carter (2014) propose ... (pp.
12–16).
Subsequent instances: Edwards et al. (2014) further described ...
(p. 15).
First instance: (Edwards, Bell, & Carter, 2014, pp. 12–16)
Subsequent instances: (Edwards et al., 2014, p. 15).

AUTHOR AND EDITOR

Author, A. (Year). *Title of book*. A. Editor (Ed.). Available from http:// www.yyyyy.com/xxxxx

Shakespeare, W. (1997). *King Lear*. R.A. Foakes (Ed.). Retrieved from Amazon.com

Adey (2014) proposes … (p. 25).
(Adey, 2014, p. 25)

ONE AUTHOR, TWO EDITORS

Author, A. (Year). *Title of book*. A. Editor & B. Editor (Eds.). Available from http://www.yyyyy.com/xxxxx

Deming, D. (2012). *The essential Deming: Leadership principles from the father of equality* (1st ed.). J. Orsini & D. Cahill (Eds.). Available from http://www.coursesmart.com/the-essential-deming-leadershi p-principles/w-edwards-deming-joyce-edited-by-orsini-diana/ dp/9780071790222#extendedauthorlist

Adey (2014) admits … (pp. 153–176).
(Adey, 2014, pp. 153–176).

TWO AUTHORS, ONE EDITOR

Author, A., & Author, B. (Year). *Title of book*. A. Editor (Ed.). Available from http://www.yyyyy.com/xxxxx

Mayhew, A. & Skeat, W. (2011). *A concise dictionary of Middle English from AD 1150 to 1580*. J. Brenden (Ed.). [Kindle version]. Retrieved from Amazon.com

Adey and Brown (2014) argue … (pp. 124–166).
(Adey & Brown, 2014, pp. 124–166)

TWO AUTHORS, TWO EDITORS

Author, A., & Author, B. (Year). *Title of book*. A. Editor & B. Editor (Eds.). Available from http://www.yyyyyy.com/xxxxx

Kerouac, J. & Ginsberg, A. (2010). *Jack Kerouac and Allen Ginsberg: The letters*. B. Morgan & D. Standford (Eds.). Retrieved from Amazon.com

Adey and Brown (2014) researched … (pp. 144–167).
(Adey & Brown, 2014, pp. 144–167)

DOI NUMBER

AUTHOR

Author, A. (Year). *Title of book*. doi:xxxxxxx/xxxxxx

Ives, E. (2009). *Lady Jane Grey: A Tudor mystery*. doi:10.1002/9781444307832

Adey (2014) propose that … (p. 15).
(Adey, 2014, p. 15).

TWO AUTHORS

Author, A., & Author, B. (Year). *Title of book*. doi:xxxxxxx/xxxxx

Hindmarch, C. & Pienkowski, M. (2008). *Land management: The hidden costs*. doi:10.1002/9780470694978

Adey and Brown (2014) researched … (p. 167).
(Adey & Brown, 2014, p. 167)

THREE AUTHORS

Author, A., Author, B., & Author C. (Year). *Title of book.* doi:xxxxxx/xxxxx

Everitt, B., Landau, S., Leese, M., & Stahl, D. (2011). *Cluster analysis* (5th ed.). doi:10.1002/9780470977811

Adey, Brown, and Carter (2014) recommend … (pp. 167–174).
(Adey, Brown, & Carter, 2014, pp. 167–174)

EDITOR

Editor, E. (Ed.). (Year). *Title of book: Subtitle of book.* doi:xxxxxxx/xxxxxx

Fishcer-Lichte, E. (Ed.). (2004). *Dionysus resurrected: Performances of Euripides' The Bacchae in a globalizing world.* doi:10.1002/9781118609774

Edwards (2014) argues that … (pp. 12–16).
(Edwards, 2014, pp. 12–16)

TWO EDITORS

Editor, A., & Editor, B. (Eds.). (Year). *Title of book.* doi:xxxxx/xxxxx

Fjeldly, M., & Shur, S. (Eds.). (2005). *Lab on the web: Running real electronics experiments via the Internet.* doi:10.1002/0471727709

Edwards and Bell (2014) propose … (p. 116).
(Edwards & Bell, 2014, p. 116)

THREE EDITORS

Editor, A., Editor, B., & Editor, C. (Eds.). (Year). *Title of book.* doi:xxxxxxx/xxxxx

Hoaglin, D., Mosteller, F., & Tukey, J. (Eds.). (2011). *Exploring data tables, trends, and shapes*. doi:10.1002/9781118150702

First, instance: Edwards, Bell, and Carter (2014) recommend ... (pp. 121–162).
Subsequent instances: Edwards et al. (2014) further described ... (p. 17).
First instance: (Edwards, Bell & Carter, 2014, pp. 121–162)
Subsequent instances: (Edwards et al., 2014, p. 17).

AUTHOR AND EDITOR

Author, A. (Year). *Title of book*. A. Editor (Ed.) doi:xxxxxxxxx/xxxxxx
Reeve, R. (2002). *Introduction to environmental analysis*. D. Ando (Ed.). doi:10.1002/0470845783

Adey (2014) argues ... (pp. 67–69).
(Adey, 2014, pp. 67–69)

CHAPTER IN A BOOK—PRINT

ONE AUTHOR, ONE EDITOR

Author, A. (Year). Title of chapter. In A. Editor (Ed.), *Title of book* (pp. xx–xx). City, ST: Publisher
Levinson, L. (1997). The clearing. In R. Echevarria (Ed.), *Oxford book of Latin American short stories* (pp. 205–110). New York, NY: Oxford Press.

Adey (2014) states ... (pp. 55–76).
(Adey, 2014, pp. 55–76)

ONE AUTHOR, TWO EDITORS

Author, A. (Year). Title of chapter. In A. Editor & B. Editor (Eds.), *Title of book* (pp. xx–xx). City, ST: Publisher

Lee, B. A job like a tattoo. (2001). In G. Savage & D. Sullivan (Eds.), *Writing a professional life: Stories of technical communicators on and off the job.* Needham Heights, MA: Allyn & Bacon.

Adey (2014) writes… (p. 86).
(Adey, 2014, p. 86)

ONE AUTHOR, THREE EDITORS

Author, A. (Year). Title of chapter. In A. Editor, B. Editor, & C. Editor (Eds.), *Title of book* (pp. xx–xx). City, ST: Publisher.

Diacu, F. (2008). The birth of celestial mechanics. In C. Davis, M. Senechal, & J. Zwicky (Eds.), *The shape of content: Creative writing in mathematics and science* (pp. 55– 76). Wellesley, MA: AK Peters, Ltd.

Adey (2014) predicts … (p 34).
(Adey, 2014, p. 34)

TWO AUTHORS, THREE EDITORS

Author, A., & Author, B. (Year). Title of chapter. In A. Editor, B. Editor & C. Editor (Eds.), *Title of book* (pp. xx–xx). City, ST: Publisher.

Jorge, R., & Robinson, R. (2011). Mood Disorders. In J. Silver, T. McAllister, & S. Yudofsky (Eds.), *Textbook of traumatic brain injury* (2nd edition) (pp. 173–189). Arlington, VA: American Psychiatric Publishing.

Adey and Brown (2014) examined … (p. 445).
(Adey & Brown, 2014, p. 445)

TWO AUTHORS, TWO EDITORS

Author, A., & Author, B. (Year). Title of chapter. In A. Editor & B. Editor (Eds.), *Title of book* (pp. xx -xx). City, ST: Publisher.

McBride, L., & Bird, E. (2011). From smart fan to backyard wrestler: performance, context, and aesthetic violence. In G. Dines & J. Humez (Eds.), *Gender, race, and class in Media: A critical reader* (pp. 583–590). Thousand Oaks, CA: SAGE Publications.

Adey and Brown (2014) observed ... (pp. 12–13).
(Adey & Brown, 2014, pp. 12–13)

THREE AUTHORS, THREE EDITORS

Author, A., Author, B., & Author, C. (Year). Title of chapter. In A. Editor, B. Editor, & C. Editor (Eds.), *Title of book* (pp. xx –xx). City, ST: Publisher.

Anderson, K., Hurley, R., & Taber, K. (2011). Functional imaging. In J. Silver, T. McAllister, & S. Yudofsky, *Textbook of traumatic brain injury* (2nd edition) (pp. 91–114). Arlington, VA: American Psychiatric Publishing.

First instance: Adey, Brown, and Cole (2014) concede that ... (pp. 34–36).
Second instance: Adey et al. (2014) further argue ... (pp. 34–36).
First instance: (Adey, Brown, & Cole, 2014, p. 111)
Subsequent instances: (Adey et al., 2014, p. 111)

AUTHOR AND EDITOR WITH TWO DIFFERENT PUBLICATION DATES

Author, A. (Year.) Title of chapter or story. In A. Editor (Ed.), Title of book (Vol. #, pp. xx–xx). Retrieved from http://www.yyyyyy.com/ xxxxx (Original work published year)

Poe, E. A. (1995). Fall of the house of Usher. In R. V. Cassill (Ed.), *The Norton Anthology of Short Fiction* (pp. 1373–1388). New York, NY: W.W. Norton & Company. (Original work published 1839)

Adey (2014) supports ... (p. 16).
(Adey, 2014, p. 16)

CHAPTER IN AN E-BOOK

WEB ADDRESS

AUTHOR AND EDITOR

Author, A. (Year). Title of chapter. In A. Editor & B. Editor (Eds.), *Title of book* (pp. xx–xx). http://www.yyyyyy.com/xxxxx

Oppen, G. (2007). Party on shipboard. In N. Baym, *The Norton anthology of American literature* (p. 2122). Retrieved from http://books.wwnorton.com/books/detail-contents.aspx?ID=10203

Adey (2014) investigated ... (pp. 14–16).
(Adey, 2014, pp. 14–16)

TWO AUTHORS, TWO EDITORS

Author, A., & Author, B. (Year). Title of chapter. In A. Editor & B. Editor (Eds.), *Title of book* (pp. xx–xx). http://www.yyyyyy.com/xxxxx

Gray, M., & Campbell, F. (2004). Urinary tract disorders. In B. Ferrell & N. Coyle, *The textbook of palliative nursing* (pp. 265–284). Retrieved from https://openlibrary.org/books/OL3296502M/Textbook_of_palliative_nursing/daisy

Adey and Brown (2014) report ... (pp. 222–223).
(Adey & Brown, 2014, pp. 222–223)

ONE AUTHOR, THREE EDITORS

Jones, B. (1987). The shadows on the lawn. In M. Greenburg, J. Lellenberg, & C. Waugh, *The new adventures of Sherlock Holmes: Original stories by eminent mystery writers* (pp. 131–160). Retrieved from https://archive.org/stream/newadventuresofs00vari#page/n3/mode/2up

Adey (2014) acknowledges ... (p. 177).
(Adey, 2014, p. 177)

THREE AUTHORS, ONE EDITOR

Colbeck, I., Baltensperger, U., & Furger, M. (2007). Aerosol chemistry in remote locations. In I. Colbeck (Ed.), *Environmental chemistry of aerosols (1ˢᵗ ed.)* (pp. 217–242). Hoboken, NJ: Wiley and Sons Publishing.

Adey (2014) observes ... (p. 17).
(Adey, 2014, p. 17)

CHAPTER IN E-BOOK—DOI

AUTHOR AND EDITOR

Author, A. (Year). Title of chapter. In A. Editor (Ed.), *Title of book* (pp. xx–xx). doi:xxxxxxx/xxxxx
Allan, W. (2007). Tragedy and the early Greek philosophical tradition. In J. Gregory, *A companion to Greek tragedy* (pp. 71–82). doi:10.1002/9780470996676.ch5

Adey (2014) notes ... (p. 174).
(Adey, 2014, p. 174)

ONE AUTHOR, TWO EDITORS

Author, A. (Year). Title of chapter. In A. Editor & B. Editor (Eds.), *Title of book*, (pp. xx–xx). doi:xxxxxxx/xxxxx

Bolnick, D. I. (2007). Hybridization and speciation in centrarchids. In S. J. Cooke & D. P. Philipp (Eds.), *Centrarchid fishes: Diversity, Biology, and conservation* (pp. 39–69). doi:10.1002/9780470262269.ch2

Adey (2014) acknowledges ... (pp. 15–21).
(Adey, 2014, pp. 15–21)

TWO AUTHORS, ONE EDITOR

Author, A., & Author, B. (Year). Title of chapter. In A. Editor (Ed.), *Title of book*, (pp. xx–xx). doi:xxxxxxx/xxxxx

Frankauser, P. & Pumain, D. (2010). Fractals and Geography. In L. Sanders (Ed.), *Models in Spatial Analysis*, (pp. 281–311). doi:10.1002/9780470612255.ch10

Adey and Brown (2014) propose ... (p. 167).
(Adey & Brown, 2014, p. 167)

TWO AUTHORS, TWO EDITORS

Author, A., & Author, B. (Year). Title of chapter. In A. Editor, & B. Editor (Eds.), *Title of book*, (pp. xx–xx). doi:xxxxxxx/xxxxx

Near, T.J., & Koppelman, J.B. (2007). Species diversity, phylogeny, and phylogeography of centrarchidae. In S. J. Cooke, & D. P. Philipp, (Eds.), *Centrarchid fishes: Diversity, Biology, and conservation* (pp. 1–38). doi:10.1002/9781444316032.ch13

Adey and Brown (2014) argue ... (pp. 267–273).
(Adey & Brown, 2014, p. 267–273)

THREE AUTHORS, ONE EDITOR

Author, A., Author, B., & Author, C. (Year). Title of chapter. In A. Editor (Ed.), *Title of book*, (pp. xx–xx). doi:xxxxxxx/xxxxx

Colbeck, I., Baltensperger, U., & Furger, M. (2009). Aerosol chemistry in remote locations. In I. Colbeck (Ed.), *Environmental chemistry of aerosols* (pp. 217–242). doi:10.1002/9781444305388.ch8

First instance: Adey, Brown, and Cole (2014) admit that … (pp. 388–391).

Second instance: Adey et al. (2014) further argue … (pp. 388–391).

First instance: (Adey, Brown, & Cole, 2014, p. 105)

Subsequent instances: (Adey et al., 2014, p. 105)

ENTRY WITH NO BYLINE (REFERENCE BOOK)

PRINT

Title of entry. (Year). In E. Editor (Ed.) Title of reference book (xx ed., Vol. xx, pp. xx–xx). Location: Publisher.

Trapper. (2001). In *Webster's New World College Dictionary* (4th Ed.). Foster City, CA: IDG Books Worldwide, Inc.

ONLINE

Title of entry. (Year.) in E. Editor (Ed.), Title of reference book (xx ed., Vol. xx, pp. xx–xx). Retrieved from http://www.yyyyy.xxx

Hackers. n. d. In *Merriam-Webster's online dictionary*. Retrieved from http://www.merriam-webster.com/dictionary/hackers

ARTICLES 〜〜〜〜〜〜〜〜〜〜〜〜〜〜

NEWSPAPER—PRINT 〜〜〜〜〜〜〜〜〜〜〜〜〜

ONE AUTHOR

Author, A. (Year, Month Date). Title of article. *Title of Newspaper*, p. x, x).

Walker, D. (2014, September 30). Task force puts price tag on cultural needs. *The Milwaukee Journal Sentinel*, pp. 1A, 4A.

Adey (2014) researched … (p. 1B).
(Adey, 2014, p. 1B)

TWO AUTHORS

Author, A., & Author, B. (Year, Month Date). Title of article. *Title of Newspaper*, p. x, x).

Gallagher, K., & Johnson, M. (2014, September 30). Medical College awarded $2.5 million grant. *The Milwaukee Journal Sentinel*, pp. 1A, 4A.

Adey and Brown (2014) researched … (p. 1A).
(Adey & Brown, 2014, p. 1A)

PRINT

Title of article. (Year, Month Date). *Title of Newspaper*, p. x.

Strong typhoons take aim in Pacific. (2014, October 6). *Milwaukee Journal Sentinel*, p. 3A.

The article "Title of Article" (2014) proposes … (para. 3).
("Title of article," 2014, paras. 3–5)

NEWSPAPER ONLINE

ONE AUTHOR

Author, A. (Year, Month Day). Title of article. *Title of Newspaper*. Retrieved from http://www.newspaperwebsite.com

Chachkevitch, A. (2014, October 6). 3 killed in 11-car pileup. *Chicago Tribune*. Retrieved from http://www.chicagotribune.com

Adey (2014) reports ... (paras. 2–4).
(Adey, 2014, paras. 2–4)

ONLINE, TWO AUTHORS

Author, A., & Author B. (Year, Month Day). Title of article. *Title of Newspaper*. Retrieved from http://www.newspaperwebsite.com

Hardy, Q. & Gelles, D. (2014, October 6). Hewlett-Packard announces breakup plan as technology landscape shifts. *New York Times*. Retrieved from http://www.nytimes.com

Adey and Brown (2014) report ... (paras. 5–7).
(Adey & Brown 2014, paras. 5–7)

ONLINE, NO AUTHOR

Title of article. (Year, Month, day). *Title of Newspaper*. Retrieved from https://www.newspaperwebsite.com

Keeping Credit Cards and Bank Account Data from Hackers (2014, October, 4). *New York Times*. Retrieved from http://www. nytimes.com

An article in the *New York Times* (2014) argues .... (para. 5).
("Title of Article," 2014, para. 5)

JOURNAL—PRINT

ONE AUTHOR

Author, A. (Year). Title of article. *Title of Journal*, Volume (Issue), xx–xx.

Rosen, M. (1985). Breakfast at Spiro's: Dramaturgy and dominance. *Journal of Management*, 11, 31–48.

Adey (2014) researched … (pp. 155–202).
(Adey, 2014, pp. 155–202)

TWO AUTHORS

Author, A., & Author, B. (Year). Title of article. *Title of Journal*, Volume (Issue), xx–xx.

Alvesson, M., & Willmott, H. (1992). On the idea of emancipation in management and organization studies. *Academy of Management Review*, 17 (3), 432–464.

Adey and Brown (2014) argue … (p. 460).
(Adey & Brown, 2014, p. 460)

JOURNAL ONLINE—DOI

The DOI number might be listed with as a web address link or just as the DOI number. Therefore, the DOI could be cited like one of these two examples:

- doi:xx.xxxxx/xxxxx
- http://dx.doi.org/10.0000/0000

ONE AUTHOR

Author, A. (Year). Title of article. *Title of Journal*, volume (issue), xx–xx. doi:xxxxxxxxxx/xxxxx

Trussler, S. (2014, August 6). Charles Marowitz in London: Twenty-five years hard: Marowitz in the Sixties. *New Theatre Quarterly*, 30 (3), 203–206. doi:10.1017/S0266464X14000402

Adey (2014) proposes … (pp. 125–256).
(Adey, 2014, pp. 125–256)

TWO AUTHORS

Author, A., & Author, B. (Year). Title of article. *Title of Journal, Volume (issue)*, xx–xx. doi:0000000/000000000000

Chintakananda, A. & McIntyre, D. (2014). Market entry in the presence of network effects: A real options perspective. *Journal of Management, 40 (15)*, 1535–1557. doi:10.1177/0149206311429861

Latiolais, M. P., & Laurence, W. (2009). Engaging math-avoidant college students. *Numeracy*, 2 (2), 5. http://dx.doi.org/10.5038/1936-4660.2.2.5

Adey and Brown (2014) acknowledge … (pp. 16–25).
(Adey & Brown, 2014, p. 16–25)

THREE AUTHORS

Author, A., Author, B., & Author, C. (Year). Title of article. *Title of Journal, Volume (issue)*, xx–xx. doi:0000000/000000000000

Dacin, M. T., Munir, K., & Tracey, P. (2010). Formal dining at Cambridge Colleges: Linking ritual performance and institutional maintenance. *Academy of Management Journal*, 53 (6), 1393–1418. doi:10.5465/AMJ.2010.57318388ACAD

Mulot, C., Stucker, I., Clavel, J., Beaune, P., & Loriot, M.A. (2005). Collection of human genomic DNA from buccal cells for genetic studies: Comparison between cytobrush, mouthwatch, and treated card. *Journal of Biomedicine and Biotechnology*, 2005 (3), 291–296. http://dx.doi.org/10.1155/JBB.2005.291

First instance: Adey, Brown, and Cole (2014) acknowledge that … (pp. 77–99).
Second instance: Adey et al. (2014) further argue … (pp. 77–99).
First instance: (Adey, Brown, & Cole, 2014, p. 100)
Subsequent instances: (Adey et al., 2014, p. 100)

JOURNAL ONLINE—WEBSITE

ONE AUTHOR

Author, A. (Year). Title of article. *Title of Journal*, Volume (Issue), xx–xx. Retrieved from http://www.website.com/xxxxxxx
Morton, T. (2009). How to obtain velocity fields from observed stream-line patterns. *Journal of Scientific and Mathematical Research*, 3, 18–28. Retrieved from http://www.jscimath.org/library/results.cfm?wherefrom=SEARCH

Adey (2014) acknowledges … (pp. 22–35).
(Adey, 2014, pp. 22–35)

TWO AUTHORS

Author, A., & Author, B. (Year). Title of article. *Title of Journal*, Volume (Issue), xx–xx. Retrieved from http://www.website.com/xxxxxxx
George, A., & Cebra, J. J. (1991). Responses of single germinal-center B. cells in T-cell-dependent microculture. *PNAS*, 88 (1), 11–15. Retrieved from http://www.pnas.org/content/88/1.toc

Adey and Brown (2014) argue … (p. 5).
(Adey & Brown, 2014, p. 5)

THREE AUTHORS

Author, A., Author, B., & Author, C. (Year). Title of article. *Title of Journal*, Volume (Issue), xx–xx. Retrieved from http://www.web-site.com/xxxxxxx

Hongying, F., Qingping, W., & Xiaoxia, K. (2008). Co-detection of five species of water-borne. *Life Science Journal*, 5 (4), 47–58. http://www.lifesciencesite.com/lsj/life0504/

First instance: Adey, Brown, and Cole (2014) predict … (pp. 8–11).
Second instance: Adey et al. (2014) further argue … (pp. 8–11).
First instance: (Adey, Brown, & Cole, 2014, p. 100)
Subsequent instances: (Adey et al., 2014, p. 100)

MAGAZINE—PRINT

NO AUTHOR

Title of article. (Year, Month). *Title of Magazine*, volume (issue), xx–xx.
Committed to collaboration. (2014, April). *Healthcare Contracting*, 11 (2), 8–11.

"Title of article," (2014) proposes … (p. 45).
("Title of article," 2014, p. 45).

(Note that for articles that have no author, you place the article title in quotes in the in-text citations, but not in the References page. This is true of all articles in newspapers, journals, magazines, and online articles.)

ONE AUTHOR

Author, A. (Year, Month). Title of article. *Title of Magazine*, volume (issue), xx –xx.

Katner, S. (2014, Fall). A billion-dollar driveway. *National Parks,* 88 (4), 36–44.

> Adey (2014) argues ... (pp. 1–10).
> (Adey, 2014, pp. 1–10)

TWO AUTHORS

Author, A., & Author, B. (Year, Month). Title of article. *Title of Magazine,* volume (issue), xx–xx.
Ash, J. M., & Golomb, S. (2004, February). Tiling deficient rectangles with trominoes. *Mathematics Magazine,* 32 (1), 46–55.

> Adey and Brown (2014) write ... (p. 165).
> (Adey & Brown, 2014, p. 165)

MAGAZINE—ONLINE

NO AUTHOR

Title of article. (Year, Month). *Title of magazine,* volume (issue), xx–xx.
Committed to Collaboration. (2014, April). *Healthcare Contracting,* 11 (2), 8–14.

> "Title of article" (2014) reports ... (p. 2).
> ("Title of article," 2014, p. 2)

(Note that for articles that have no author, you place the article title in quotes in the in-text citations—but not in the References page. This is true of all articles in newspapers, journals, magazines, and online articles.)

ONE AUTHOR

Author, A. (Year, Month). Title of article. *Title of Magazine*, volume (issue), xx –xx. Retrieved from http://www.magwebsite.com/xxxxx

Bastone, Kelly. (2014, August.) One night wonders. *Backpacker Magazine*, 5, 58–67. Retrieved from http://www.zinio.com/www/browse/issue.jsp?skuId=416269721&prnt=&offer=&or

Adey (2014) states ... (p. 16).

(Adey, 2014, p. 16)

TWO AUTHORS

Author, A., & Author, B. (Year, Month). Title of article. *Title of Magazine*, volume (issue), xx–xx. Retrieved from http://www.yyyyy.com/xxx

Ratcliffe, M., & Ling, A. (2014, November). November 2014: Mercury in the morning. *Astronomy*, 42 (11), 36–44. Available from http://www.zinio.com/reader.jsp?issue=416316045&e=true

Adey and Brown (2014) discovered ... (pp. 18–22).

(Adey & Brown, 2014, pp. 18–22)

WEB ARTICLE

NO AUTHOR

Title of article. (Year). Retrieved Month, Day, Year, from http://www.website.com/xxxxxxx

How do you reference a web page that lists no author? (2010). Retrieved October 7, 2014 from http://www.apastyle.org/learn/faqs/web-page-no-author.aspx

"Title of article" (2014) reports ... (paras. 6–9).
("Title of article," 2014, paras. 6–9)

(Note that for articles that have no author, you place the article title in quotes in the in-text citations—but not in the References page. This is true of all articles in newspapers, journals, magazines, and online articles.)

AUTHOR

Author, A. (Year.) Title of article. Retrieved Month, Day, Year from
    http://www.website.org/xxxxxx
Norton, A. (2014, September 24). Varicose vein treatments all work, but ...
    study found minor differences between three therapies. Retrieved
    October 8, 2014 from http://www.webmd.com/skin-problems-and-
    treatments/news/20140924/varicose-vein-treatments-all-work-
    but-arent-quite-equal

Norton (2014) asserts ... (para. 7)
(Norton, 2014, para. 7)

ORGANIZATION AS AUTHOR

Title of Organization. (Year, Day, Month). Title of article. Retrieved
    from http://www.website.org/xxxxx
American Heart Association. (2014, September 15). About arrhythmia.
    Retrieved from http://www.heart.org/HEARTORG/Conditions/
    Arrhythmia/AboutArrhythmia/About-Arrhythmia_UCM_
    002010_Article.jsp

First instance: The American heart Association (2014) warns ...
(para. 4).
Subsequent instances: The AHA (2014) also warns ... (para. 7).

First Instance: (The American Heart Association, 2014, para. 4).
Subsequent instances: (AHA, 2014, para. 7)

PODCAST

ONE PRODUCER

Producer, A. (Year, Month, Day). Title of episode [#]. Name of Podcast.
  Retrieved from http://www.webaddress.com/xxxxx
Updike, N. (2014, September 5). It's not the product, it's the person [533]. This American Life from WBEZ. Retrieved from
  http://www.thisamericanlife.org/radio-archives/episode/533/
  its-not-the-product-its-the-person

Producer (2014) discusses ...
(Producer, 2014)

TWO PRODUCERS

Producer, A., & Producer B. (Year, Month, Day). Title of episode [#].
  Name of Podcast. Retrieved from http://www.webaddress.com/
  xxxxx
Cole, S., & Calhoun, B. (Producers). (2014,). A not-so-simple majority
  [534]. This American Life from WBEZ. Retrieved from http://www.
  thisamericanlife.org/radio-archives/episode/534/a-not-so-simple-
  majority

Producer and Producer (2014) provide ...
(Producer & Producer 2014)

BLOG POST

Author, A. (Year, Month, Day). Title of article [Web log message]. Retrieved from http://www.yyyyy.com/xxx

Lawler, R. (2014, October 8). Enterprise Collaboration Startup Slack Blames Admins For Making Team Names Visible [Web log message]. Retrieved from http://techcrunch.com/2014/10/08/slack-team-names/

Lawler (2014) supports ... (paras. 4–6).
(Lawler, 2014, paras. 4–6)

PDF/POWERPOINT DOCUMENTS

Author, A. (Year). Title of document [Type of document]. Retrieved from http:/www.website.com/xxxxx

Merkely, G., & Allen, R. Center Pivot Uniformity Evaluation [PDF document]. Retrieved from http://ocw.usu.edu/Biological and Irrigation Engineering/SprinkleTrickle Irrigation/6110 L14 Center Pivot Uniformity Evaluation.pdf

Adey (2014) proposes ... (p. 2).
(Adey, 2014, p. 2)

LONG QUOTES

Long quotes are set up slightly differently than short quotes. A long quote is considered forty or more words. These should be used sparingly throughout your essay. This example shows how to use a long quote with one author. For multiple authors or editors, see the section of the quick reference guide.

THE MOST COMMON FORMAT STYLE FOR A LONG QUOTE

Use the author's name in the introductory text by stating that Adey (2014) argues:

> Your quote should use the exact words that you found in the text. Note there are no quotation marks for long quotes. This is because the use of tabs indicates this is a long quote. However, don't forget you should still use the author-date format and put the paragraph or page numbers at the end. This example shows how to set up a long quote if you use the author in the introductory text. (p. 35)

APA STYLE RESEARCH ESSAY EXAMPLE

Saving America's Infrastructure

Beth Lee

Southern New Hampshire University

During an otherwise normal rush hour, Bridge 9340 (The Mississippi River Bridge that took passengers across on I-35W), collapsed, killing 13 people and injuring another 145 people. The Star Tribune reported that "Federal regulators blamed the disaster on improperly designed gusset plates for steel beams that fell when the bridge was heavily loaded with construction equipment. They also cited inadequate attention to the plates by state and federal officials during inspections," (Doyle, 2014, para. 10). The failure of this bridge, one of the worst disasters of its day, highlights the infrastructure problems prevalent in America's bridges, water supplies and roadways, waterways and aviation. We must ask ourselves, why are infrastructures left to fail, leaving structures and roadways in ruin and lives at stake? The answer is not so simple. In order to ensure a safer infrastructure in America, three things are necessary: 1) funding from both private and government sectors, 2) bipartisan support, and 3) more workers to rebuild the structures.

In 1817, a congressman by the name of John Calhoun urged 'his fellow congressmen to 'bind the Republic together with a perfect system of roads and canals.'" Later, FDR signed the New Deal to government, allowing for programs that helped a boom in the building of America's infrastructure. Even later, in 1955, Eisenhower argued "that a modern, efficient highway system is essential to meet the needs of our growing population, our expanding economy, and our national security" (White, 2012, para. 2). Today, those roadways, bridges, waterways, aviation, and water sources are in deep need of repair. If they are not, it is almost a surety that there will be more failures in our infrastructure system.

The first approach to ensuring that America's infrastructure needs to be repaired is procuring funding from both private and government sectors. The gap between what funding is available and what will be made available for the short term is vastly disparate, and unless funds are more readily available, there won't be much progress made to fix the aging infrastructure. In 2012, the Department of Transportation's federal capital spending was $73 billion, which covered funding bridges, roads, waterways, aviation and partial operating costs. Unfortunately, this funding meets only about half of the need for roadways (Hargreaves, 2013, paras. 2–6). However, while this funding was used for vitally important projects to our infrastructure, it is not nearly the amount of money needed to meet the necessary repairs for major projects.

In fact, that $73 million is very short of the estimated cost of reparation to bridges, roadways, aviation, railways, busses, waterways and other structures in need of replacement or repair. According to the American Society of Civil Engineers (ASCE), America is currently receiving a D+ on its infrastructure upkeep. The amount needed to fix our infrastructure is an estimated $3.6 trillion by the year 2020

(American Society of Civil Engineers [ASCE], 2014). The ASCE boasts more than 145,000 members nationwide and is the foremost expert group on how our infrastructure does or does not function ("How Many Members?" 2014). If this money is not spent, the ASCE predicts that more than $1 trillion will be lost in lost business, and as many as 3.5 million jobs will also be lost (Hargreaves, 2013, para. 8). If infrastructures fail, people will be unable to readily move from one place to another, making it more difficult to get to their jobs, doctors, grocers, retailers, family and friends' homes, and other destinations. If, for instance, a bridge fails, businesses could close because of the lack of access.

If the government funding remains short, where does that leave funding? More and more, funding has gone to the private sector. As of 2011, there were " at least 70 privately funded and managed infrastructure projects across the United States in various stages of development, according to a list compiled by the law firm Allen & Overy" (Podkul, 2011, para. 6). Of these private funds, $180 billion have come from the largest 30 investors. At the beginning of the new millennium, virtually no private funding existed for infrastructure rebuild. Today, it is seen as investment because everyone needs water, to drive the streets, to use bridges to cross waterways. Investors assume there will be a clear return on their investment (Podkul, 2011, paras. 14–18).

In order for funding to continue, and even to be increased, all political parties must be in agreement on the importance of the matter. Bracken Hendricks, senior fellow at the Center for American Progress and specialist in energy and infrastructure states that "rebuilding America's infrastructure is a top-tier issue that should be able to achieve bipartisan support ….Mayors and governors need help, local industries are threatened, the banks aren't lending, and government budgets are tapped" (Hargreaves, 2013, para. 14). Kane and Puentes (2014) argue that "the federal role of the infrastructure is overemphasized" (para. 5).

In addition to more funding, the federal government could do more to facilitate the repairs to the failing infrastructures. For instance, both parties could agree to offer more low cost loans to each state, and set more national policies that will allow states and private business to make the necessary repairs (Puentes and Katz, 2014, paras. 14–15). Bipartisan agreement would lessen the red tape needed to set policies in Washington, which will lead to necessary repairs before failure to them occurs. It could also lead to more state and local control and thereby putting more responsibility on state governments.

As it turns out Ritzholz (2014) reports, "there is only a small gap between what the liberal left and the reasonable right are both advocating for when it comes to infrastructure" (para. 10). While the solutions are not as readily resolved as bipartisan support, and much needs to happen following the passing of policies, it is a much needed stop in the right direction. How much time do we have before another failure occurs, putting people's lives at stake?

The bad news is that as of September 2012, unemployment rate in America was 8.2%, making new jobs a necessity for a healthy economy (United States Department of Labor, 2014). The good news is that if more jobs were created for rebuilding America's infrastructure, these jobs would be readily available to people without college degrees, ensuring that that jobs can go to the working, middle classes. In fact, 11% of Americans are employed in jobs related to infrastructure, and of those, only 12% hold a Bachelor's degree or higher (Kane & Puentes, 2014, paras. 1–3). Estimates are that by 2022, the employment in infrastructure fields will grow more than 9%. This number could be much higher when jobs are filled due to retirement and other career changes (Kane & Puentes, 2014, para. 3). With the private funding going into infrastructure and new jobs created, this will also boost our economy, in addition to reducing unemployment rates.

Since the grade for America is currently in the D range, making it a near failure, it is imperative that America make drastic and rapid changes to repair our infrastructure. This will only occur if funding becomes available from both government and private sources. In addition, Congress and the Senate must acquire a bipartisan approach to passing new laws and policies that will make it easier for reparations to be made. Once policies are made and funding becomes available, more jobs will be available to boost the economy, in addition to revamping our infrastructure. After all, as President Roosevelt said, "It is only through labor and painful effort, by grim energy and resolute courage, that we move on to better things" (Theodore Roosevelt quotes, n. d.).

REFERENCES

American Society of Civil Engineers. (2014). Launch the report card. Retrieved from http://www.infrastructurereportcard.org/

Doyle, P. (2014, July 27). I-35W bridge is aging, seven years after collapse. *Star Tribune*. Retrieved from http://www.startribune.com/politics/statelocal/268746561.html

How many members are there? (2013, September 30). Retrieved from http://www.asce.org/Content.aspx?id=7217

Hargreaves, S. (2013, February 13). The high cost of America's bad roads and bridges. *CNN*. Retrieved from http://money.cnn.com/2013/02/12/news/economy/infrastructure-pending/

Kane, J. & Puentes, R. (2014, May 4). Summary of findings. *Brookings*. Retrieved from http://www.brookings.edu/research/interactives/2014/infrastructure-jobs#/M10420

Podkul, C. (2011, October 22). With U.S. infrastructure aging, public funds scant, more projects going private. *The Washington Post*. Retrieved from http://www.washingtonpost.com/business/with-u s-infrastructure-aging-public-funds-scant-more-projects-going-private/2011/10/17/gIQAGTuv4L_story.html

Puentes, R., & Katz, B. (2014, May 9). To fix America's infrastructure, Washington needs to get out of the way. *Forbes*. Retrieved from http://www.forbes.com/sites/realspin/2014/05/09/to-fix-america s-infrastructure-washington-needs-to-get-out-of-the-way/

Ritzholz, B. (2014, August 29). Conservatives learn to love infrastructure. Bloomberg. Retrieved from http://www.bloombergview.com/articles/2014-08-29/conservatives-learn-to-love-infrastructure

Theodore Roosevelt quotes. (n. d.) Retrieved from http://www.brainyquote.com/quotes/quotes/t/theodorero147887.html#WIlGPsETYwQrS450.99

United States Department of Labor: Bureau of Labor Statistics. (2014, October 14). Databases, tables & calculators by subject. Retrieved from http://data.bls.gov/timeseries/LNS14000000

White, A. (2012). Infrastructure policy: Lessons from American history. *The New Atlantis*. Retrieved from http://www.thenewatlantis.com/publications/infrastructure-policy-lessons-from-american-history

~~~~~~

APA. American Psychological Association.

APA Publication Manual of the American Psychological Association. A style manual written and published by the American Psychological Association.

APA Style formatting. An academic format with a set of guidelines adopted by the American Psychological Association that is used by scholars publishing in the social sciences, colleges, and high schools.

Apastyle.org. The website sanctioned by the American Psychological Association.

Chicago Manual of Style. A set of formatting guidelines adopted by the history, humanities, and the arts for citing sources. It is widely used in newspaper and other forms of publishing.

citation. A method of telling your reader more information about your source. The APA Style formatting uses an author-date method for citations.

common knowledge. Knowledge that you can expect most people will already know. For instance, it would be common knowledge to state that Benjamin Franklin discovered electricity.

dissertation. The dissertation is an academic publication of your findings and academic pursuits that is usually a mandatory process in earning a doctoral degree. The dissertation is generally presented to a panel of academics (and is open to the public) at the end of your studies prior to graduation.

DOI number. A digital object identifier is a unique number that is assigned to a journal or book. Not all journals and books currently have DOI numbers attached. If a journal or book title has a DOI number attached, it should always be used in the References page entry of your research essay.

Easybib. An online service that helps students create citations for their academic research essays. As of this writing, APA Style formatting was a paid service.

e-book. A book in electronic format, such as a Kindle or PDF.

format. A way to conform to the guidelines set forth by your instructor or professor when writing an academic research essay.

in-text citations. A method of reporting your research sources in a parenthetical format within the essay itself. The APA Style uses the author-date method of in-text citations. Every in-text citation needs to have an entry in the References page at the end of your essay.

ISBN number. Short for International Standard Book Number, the ISBN is a thirteen-digit code given to all published books as a way of universally identifying the book.

mechanics. Mechanics refers to the "boring" part of writing your essay papers. It encompasses the nitty-gritty or technical aspects of the writing process. For the purposes of this book, mechanics refers to grammar (punctuation, spelling, etc.), voice, tone, clarity, and conciseness of your writing.

MLA Style Manual. Modern Language Association, which is a style guide for research that is used mostly in the humanities and liberal arts.

plagiarism. Using someone else's ideas, thoughts, or words and taking credit for them. Don't do this. It's wrong—and you could get in a lot of trouble for it.

primary source. The primary source is a document (or taped interview) that was written (or recorded) during the time period, such as a diary, speech, news footage, letter, or creative work. One of the most infamous primary sources is *The Diary of Anne Frank*.

Purdue's OWL. The OWL is Purdue University's online writing lab. It is accessible and a free service to anyone; it hosts writing resources and instructional materials. (There is a physical writing lab accessible only to Purdue students.)

References page. A separate page or pages at the end of your essay that includes an entry for each outside source cited in the essay. It follows a very specific set of formatting guidelines. (No, you cannot just post websites as your entry.) Each entry in the References page should match an in-text citation from the essay.

secondary source. Secondary sources interpret and analyze primary sources that were written after the event that occurred. This is what most of you will be working with in your academic careers. They are newspapers, book, journals, criticisms, encyclopedias, commentaries, etc.

source. Where you received your information. This might come in the form of a book, journal, newspaper, magazine, website, interview, or legal statute. There are generally two types: primary and secondary.

OWL. Purdue's online writing lab is accessible to anyone and has resources for students to gain greater knowledge of most subjects related to research writing and grammar.

thesis. The thesis is an academic publication of your findings and academic pursuits that is usually a mandatory process in earning a master's degree (though a capstone project is sometimes allowed.) The thesis is generally presented to a panel of academics (and is also open to the public) at the end of your studies prior to graduation.

thesis statement. The thesis statement is the road map to your essay. The thesis statement tells the reader what type of essay it is, what the essay is about, and what topics will be covered in your essay.

Turnitin (turnitin.org). Turnitin is an online plagiarism checker used by institutions worldwide. Professors and students can get access to it through their schools. It works by "running" an essay or other piece of writing through the system. The system tells the user what the likelihood that pieces or portions of the piece are plagiarized. (While you might not have access to Turnitin as a student, your professor might.)

SOURCE #1: MAIN IDEA/QUOTE

Author/Editor/ Organization Name(s)	Book/Journal/ Newspaper Title	Article Title
Publication Date	Publishing House	Page/Paragraph #
Web Address or DOI Number		

SOURCE #2: MAIN IDEA/QUOTE

Author/Editor/ Organization Name(s)	Book/Journal/ Newspaper Title	Article Title
Publication Date	Publishing House	Page/Paragraph #
Web Address or DOI number		

FURTHER RESOURCES FOR APA STYLE FORMATTING

Purdue's OWL: https://owl.english.purdue.edu/owl/resource/560/01/

APA Style Blog: http://blog.apastyle.org/

APA Style Quick Answers Guide: http://www.apastyle.org/learn/
quick-guide-on-references.aspx

APA Style: Basics of APA Style Tutorial: http://flash1r.apa.org/apa-
style/basics/index.htm

YouTube: APA Format Citations-Sixth (6th) Edition by David Taylor:
https://www.youtube.com/watch?v=9pbUoNa5tyY

YouTube: APA Research Paper: How to Write an APA Essay with
Sources by David Taylor: https://www.youtube.com/watch?v=
X6ywA8C0SDo

ProQuest: http://www.proquest.com/

ProQuest LibGuides: http://proquest.libguides.com/home

REFERENCES

About citations. (n. d.) Retrieved from http://libguides.mit.edu/citing

About Sioux Falls. (2014). Retrieved from http://visitsiouxfalls.com/visitors/about-sioux-falls//

American Psychological Association. (2012). *Publication Manual of the American Psychological Association* (6ᵗʰ ed.). Washington, DC: Author.

Angeli, E., Wagner, J., Lawrick, E., Moore, K., Anderson, M., Soderlund, L., & Brizee, A. (2010, May 5). *General Format.* Retrieved from http://owl.english.purdue.edu/owl/resource/560/01/

APA Reference Style: Introduction. (2002, Oct. 7). Retrieved from http://linguistics.byu.edu/faculty/henrichsenl/apa/APA02.html

Becker, D. (2014). When to include retrieval dates for online sources. Retrieved from http://blog.apastyle.org/apastyle/2014/08/when-to-include-retrieval-dates-for-online-sources.html

Bradbury, Ray. (1962). *Something Wicked This Way Comes.* New York, NY: Simon & Schuster.

Chamberlain, Wayne. (2014). "The True Story of the Paul Bunyan Legend." Retrieved from http://www.paulbunyanscenicbyway.org/The_True_Story_of_the_Paul_Bunyan_Legend

Complaints about APA style. (2011, October 9). Retrieved from http://www.apastyletemplate.com/apa-style/page/2/

DOI Handbook. (2013, Nov. 13). Retrieved from http://www.doi.org/doi_handbook/1_Introduction.html

Drake, Barbara. (1982). *Writing Poetry.* New York, NY: Harcourt Brace Jovanovich.

Facts about dreaming. (2016). Retrieved from http://www.webmd.
com/sleep-disorders/guide/dreaming-overview#1

Factsheet: DOI System and the ISBN System. (2012). Retrieved from
http://www.doi.org/factsheets/ISBN-A.html

Flynn, Gillian. (2012). *Gone Girl*. New York, NY: Crown Publishing.

Frequently asked questions about the DOI system. (2014, July 15).
Retrieved from http://www.doi.org/faq.html

Great educational quotes. (2014). Retrieved from http://learningrevo-
lution.com/page/great-educational-quotes

How do you cite a Reference to a Book when there is no author or
editor. (2010). Retrieved from http://www.apastyle.org/learn/faqs/
cite-book-no-author.aspx

Hunter, Judy. (2013). *The Importance of Citation* [PDF document].
Retrieved from: http://web.grinnell.edu/Dean/Tutorial/EUS/
IC.pdf

In-Text citations: Author/authors. (2014). Retrieved from https://owl.
english.purdue.edu/owl/resource/560/03/

Jacques Pepin quotes. (n. d.) Retrieved from http://www.brainyquote.
com/quotes/authors/j/jacques_pepin.html

Johnson-Sheehan, R. & Paine, C. (2013). *Writing today* (2nd ed.).
Newark, NJ: Pearson.

Kreiger, Elizabeth. (2014, June 23). Snooze news: What is sleep den-
tistry? Retrieved from http://www.webmd.com/oral-health/
features/sleep-dentistry

Larry, D., Seinfeld, J., & Andy Cowan (Writers.) (1994, 19 May). The
opposite. Shapiro, G. (Executive Producer), *Seinfeld*. New York,
NY: Shapiro/West Productions & Castle Rock Entertainment.

Leclerc, C. & Kensinger, E. Sample one experiment paper: Effects of age
on detection of emotional information.[PDF Document]. Retrieved
from apastyle.org http://supp.apa.org/style/PM6E-Corrected-
Sample-Papers.pdf

Lee, C. (2009). How do I cite a Kindle? [Blog post]. Retrieved from
http://blog.apastyle.org/apastyle/2009/09/how-do-i-cite-a-kindle.
html

McAdoo, Timothy. (2013, June 14). Block quotations in APA style. [Blog post]. Retrieved from http://blog.apastyle.org/apastyle/2013/06/block-quotations-in-apa-style.html

McMillen, M. (2014, August 20). *Alzheimer's: The state of prevention, treatment.* [Web MD log post.] Retrieved August 20, 2014 from http://blogs.webmd.com/breaking-news/2014/08/alzheimers-the-state-of-prevention-treatment.html

Narcolepsy fact sheet. (2014, April 16). Retrieved from http://www.ninds.nih.gov/disorders/narcolepsy/detail_narcolepsy.htm#261173201

Paiz, J., Angeli, E. Wagner, J. Lawrick, E. Moore, K. Anderson, ... Keck, R. (2014, August 8). Reference List: Electronic Sources (Web Publications.) Retrieved from https://owl.english.purdue.edu/owl/resource/560/10/

Paiz, J., Angeli, E. Wagner, J. Lawrick, E. Moore, K. Anderson, ... Keck, R. (2014, October 26). APA Stylistics: Basics (Web Publications.) Retrieved from https://owl.english.purdue.edu/owl/resource/560/15/

plagiarism. n. d. In *Merriam-Webster's online dictionary.* Retrieved from http://www.merriam-webster.com/dictionary/plagiarism

Poppano, Laura. (2012, November 2). The year of the MOOC. *New York Times.* Retrieved from http://www.nytimes.com/2012/11/04/education/edlife/massive-open-online-courses-are-multiplying-at-a-rapid-pace.html?pagewanted=all&_r=0

Publication Manual of the American Psychological Association (sixth ed.) (2010). Washington, D.C.: American Psychological Association.

Quick answers: Formatting. (2014). Retrieved from http://www.apastyle.org/learn/quick-guide-on-formatting.aspx

References list: Basic rules. (2013, March 1). Retrieved from https://owl.english.purdue.edu/owl/resource/560/05/

Roen, D., Glau, G., & Maid, B. (2011). *The McGraw-Hill Guide: Writing for College, Writing for Life* (2nd ed. New York, NY: McGraw-Hill.

Russel, T., Brizee, A., Angeli, E. Keck, R., & Paiz, J. (2014). MLA formatting and style guide. Retrieved from https://owl.english.purdue.edu/owl/resource/747/01/

The Story of Johnny Appleseed: Fact vs. legend. (n. d.) Retrieved from http://www.bestapples.com/kids/teachers/johnny.shtml

Weber, R., & Hurm, N. (2013, February 27). Conciseness. (Web Publications). Retrieved from https://owl.english.purdue.edu/owl/resource/572/01/

What is APA style? (2014). Retrieved from http://www.apastyle.org/learn/faqs/what-is-apa-style.aspx

What is MLA Style? (2014). Retrieved from http://www.mla.org/style

Why citing is Important. (n. d.) Retrieved from http://libguides.mit.edu/citing

What is a digital object identifier (DOI)? (2014). Retrieved from http://www.apastyle.org/learn/faqs/what-is-doi.aspx